THE WISDOM OF THE DOUBTER

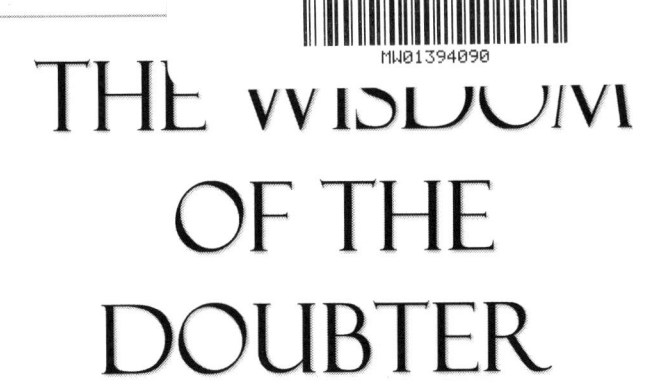

YVES CADOUX

Copyright © 2019 by Yves Cadoux

All rights reserved. This book or parts thereof may not be reproduced, stored in a retrieval system, or transmitted except in the case of brief, properly credited quotations in articles or reviews.

ISBN: 9781675566299

The author can be reached via his website: www.hylieros.com

Cover image: *Le Sauveur* by Pascal Adolphe Jean Dagnan-Bouveret

CONTENTS:

PREAMBLE	1
THE LOGIA	6
APPENDIX 1: Jesus, Thomas, and the disciples	191
APPENDIX 2: The Archons	195
GLOSSARY	199

"Take wing, my Soule, and mount up higher

For, Earth, fulfills not my Desire."

—George Wither

PREAMBLE

Dear Dominique.

Even after so many years of silence, I had not lost confidence news from you would come in time. Our bond is Sophia, and I always thought the wisdom you seek would lead you back to where your quest began. You were so willful to learn the things disdained by your elders who preferred to concern themselves with the ways of the world. You are one of those who do not belong—the pneumatici—whose destiny is to forgo all destinations. I believed you would read and conserve my letters, and that my words would remain with you, becoming companions on your solitary travels and offering a measure of light on your own discoveries. Now, with much joy I hear you keep a keen intellect in a healthy body, and I realize your erudition has exceeded my expectations. You unveiled wonders beyond the reach of the psychici who are content to heed precepts, codes, rules, dogma, and commandments, or vapidities for as long as it assuages their fears, comforts them amid doubt, and distances them ever farther from facing their utter aloneness in a hostile universe.

You learned more in your youth than I was able to gather in a lifetime. Yet, out of affectionate deference, or perhaps wondering if an old misanthrope might still be holding a handful of missing pieces to the puzzle of our existence, you ask me to elucidate the Gospel of Thomas of which you are very fond. You are well aware my young friend that is a bait I could not resist.

I was hoping to see you in person before you embark on your next journey, but I recognize your mind is steady and clear, and you must follow the thread Clotho has spun for you. May this resolve steer you again one day, if only so briefly, to sit by my side as you once did; only this time I will be the one listening attentively, and the insights you share I will collect to illumine the night before me.

* * *

Never in centuries past has there been a dearth of religious imagination, a paucity of epiphanic relevance as we experience nowadays. The abundant metaphysical harvest of the ancients has been reduced to a crop of beliefs and creeds to feed the masses a heavy meal that causes their souls to sink into a slumber. A veil of amorphous spirituality has fallen upon us, and through its diaphanous folds we perceive the deformed figures we take for the true gods. But those gods are only pretenders who hide behind the curtain and sustain our illusion of being awake while we are asleep.

In the 4th century C.E. a handful of clear-sighted monastic librarians buried a collection of manuscripts in the desert, saving them from the clutch of the engineers of faith in their time. The eremitic scholars foresaw the day when truth would "sprout up from the ground" (Psalm

85:11) to oppose the masters of delusion. When the twelve leather-bound papyrus codices concealed by the monks were found at last in 1945, the *Gospel According to Thomas* proved to be perhaps the most potent sacred text that could revive divine possession, free the mind from confusion, and rouse the soul from her torpor in our epoch.

Yet, curiosity about the intriguing wisdom of Thomas steadily waned in recent years after an initial burst of interest following the release of the logia to the general public. This is not surprising: although the promises of these ancient writings are lofty, the rewards necessitate sacrifices few are willing to offer. Unsteady seekers prefer to fall back on the comfort of books that tell them what they want to hear. What is more, Thomas' insights have been tackled mostly by academicians whose perspective buries anew the spirit of the codex.

No one ever sat at the feet of Jesus, transcribing faithfully every word that fell from his mouth. The gospel of Thomas is a collection of somewhat disparate considerations influenced by pagan, Judaic, early Christian, and Gnostic contemplative traditions. The coherence of the text comes from the thread of meaning the original redactor(s) attempted to superimpose onto the whole compilation. (And for that same reason, it is difficult to understand the logia in isolation. They illumine each other and form a tapestry as a whole. A single logion often contains the clues that will clarify the others.) Unfortunately, that meaning is largely lost to us together with the remembrance of its author(s). Yet, the spirit that animated the ancient thinkers and writers dwells in the modern reader as well, and we can draw from the same inexhaustible, unmediated source of inspiration on which they relied to ascribe our own relevant meaning to the words before us.

Because of the superimposition of new dualist and gnostic meaning onto what originally might have been mostly moral sayings, the gospel of Thomas can be understood both exoterically and esoterically. It requires a flexible mind to switch from the one to the other, sometimes within a single verse, and to rise above seeming contradictions. Indeed, this *double entendre* is a common characteristic of ancient esoteric texts that did not rely on the logical, linear processes to which we are accustomed in our time. Perhaps that is the reason we are losing touch with the ineffable that cannot be reveal logically but only through vivid images, similes and metaphors.

Our purpose then should not be to recover the original intent of the thoughts gathered in the writings of Thomas by long forgotten mystics and philosophers—an impossible task—but rather, we need to approach the text as a template to retrace the contemplative steps of the author(s). Using the sayings as a springboard, we can leap into the depths of our own being—the chasm where truth has its source.

In the *Wisdom of the Doubter*, we will endeavor to decipher Thomas' gospel on its own terms to "give birth to the one within ourselves who will save us" (see Logion 70).

Breaking through the confines of archeology, history, and textual analysis, we will journey beyond the rigor of dry academic studies onto the more fruitful, intuitive pathways of gnosis, taking the "veiled words spoken by the living Jesus" as our road signs.

May the wisdom of Thomas speak to the truthful hearts where it can deposit its secrets.

* * *

Brackets [...] in a logion indicate missing or reconstructed text from the original manuscript. Parentheses (...) suggest additional or alternative text. Underlining indicates text from the Oxyrhynchus Greek Fragments when it significantly adds meaning to the Coptic version of a logion.

A cross symbol (†) refers to a note following the commentary. **Bold characters** refer to the glossary at the end of the book.

My version of the sayings of Thomas is based on the most scholarly translations currently available. Unless otherwise noted, all biblical references are from the King James Version.

THE LOGIA

Veiled Sayings - Logion 0

> *These are the veiled words spoken by the living Jesus and written down by Judas Thomas called Didymos.*

Whence do we come? What are we? Whither do we go? Is our essence whole and unchanging or do we have an intangible nature that is polymorphic and evolving? The pithy sayings of the *Gospel according to Thomas* answer these, and many more paramount questions. It is impossible to recover the original intent of the "veiled words" lost as it is amidst the emendations of successive scribes who copied and interpreted the words, interpolating their ideas in the text when opportune. The book, as we have it today, is even more adulterated through the translation of Coptic into modern day Western languages. Yet, the function of the veiled words Thomas wrote down stays the same: to elicit a change in our ways of thinking and prompt us to access the same source of insight from which Thomas was drawing.

The incipit of the gospel introduces us to two interlocutors: Jesus and Thomas. Whether these two individuals ever existed is irrelevant. To draw the greater benefits from Thomas' words of wisdom, we need to understand Jesus, Thomas, and the disciples as allegorical figures (see also Appendix 1) standing for our own selves: they represent aspects and layers of what we are.

Thomas refers to Jesus as "the living" (†) to distinguish the living image (**eidolon**) in the heart of the *pneumatici* from the crucified god of the *psychici*. Jesus in that sense is the *syzygos*, once a mere parcel of **pneuma** in us, now the guide and savior of those who seek and listen to the hidden knowledge (hence the recurring expressions "he who has an ear to lend, let him listen).

Thomas personifies the **soul** searching for the guiding light of her *syzygos* and sharing with other willing souls the gnosis he received. He is a doubter in the canonical gospel of John (see John 20:24-29) but, unlike Peter, he is not unsteady or wavering: he must doubt everything and question all things before the truth can be manifested. It is always doubt, not faith, that is at the origin of genuine spiritual insight. Faith is the relinquishing of knowledge, whereas doubt is the threshold of knowing. The man of faith decides what God is not and accept that which he does not know about the creator. The man of gnosis seeks to understand himself to comprehend the nature of God.

Both Thomas (Semitic) and Didymos (Greek) means "twin," because the soul's image reflected in the depth grows into the likeness of a **savior twin** who becomes her companion to free her from the shackles of matter. Thomas is twin to Jesus (literally in some traditions) as Soul is twin to her living eidolon. We are the similitude of Thomas when we heed the wisdom of his gospel and set forth on a resolute path of self-discovery until we comprehend our divine nature (see Logion 2).

The disciples who hear the message of Jesus stand for the readers of the Gospel of Thomas. By and large, they (we) fail to grasp the import of its wisdom and trade the sacred knowledge in their (our) own heart for the precepts of self-appointed, all too human teachers. (See also Appendix 1).

The work of Thomas is above all a treatise on duality: not the misconstrued, mythological dualities of light and darkness or good versus evil, but those of movement and **stasis**, essence and physicality, permanence and death, **psychic thrust** and entropy, which underlie our existence.

God has been poetically likened to an infinite sphere whose center is everywhere and whose circumference is nowhere. The extraordinary thing about this proposition (apart from the fact it is perpetually misattributed) is that no one sees its most glaring implication: if some think of the divine as One and others find the "All" in multiplicity, the unknown author of the aforementioned axiom indirectly affirms the dichotomy of the whole, part circumference and part center. Being in the image of God, our divine nature too is **dyadic**: we have a soul and a *syzygos*, always separate and yet unconceivable separately, searching for each other, merging and withdrawing; savior and liberator coming together as one to free themselves from the world of matter.

For convenience, the compilation of sayings in the work of Thomas is termed a "gospel" (††) although nowhere in the original manuscript is it mentioned as such. The saying themselves are generally called "logia" and sometimes compared to the meditations of the *Tao Te Ching* or to Zen kōans. Their relevance is that of oracles: divine revelations in the form of riddles and cryptic insights pronounced by a seer (also called an "oracle") and offered at the request of the seeker for his or her benefit and enlightenment. From the context it appears that the philosophical bites, parables, and aphorisms that compose the Gospel of Thomas were not part of a missionary effort or dispensed to large crowds of followers. They were transmitted privately to close disciples occasionally mentioned by their names: James, Peter, Matthew, Mary, Salome. These oracles were pronounced to lift a corner of the veil for everyone who aspire to self-knowledge, but they will yield their secrets only before those who seek in earnest. We must heed those sacred words as if they were revealed to us individually and intimately.

—

† More precisely, the expression can refer to two separate, yet linked beings of whom Jesus is an allegorical representation. Both carry the notion of being spiritually alive as opposed to humankind at large who is spiritually dead. One is the gnostic person ("he who lives"), the dualist mystic who has awakened to salvific knowledge (see Logia 11 and 56); the other is the living eidolon (the "living one") in the heart of said gnostic: the *syzygos*, dweller in the innermost (see Logion 3:1). Through the

agency of their savior twin, the souls of the *gnostici* earn an eternal life when all else perishes in physical death (see Logion 1).

†† The term "Gospel" was not applied until the second century to books whose real authors remain anonymous to this day.

The End of Death - Logion 1

And he said: "Whoever unveils the meaning of these words will not taste death."

Life is death! The **divine essence** is entombed in the physical world. However, to die to the material reality is not of necessity to come alive in a spiritual one—be it heaven, hell, or some other netherworld—as is commonly believed. Unless the soul and her savior twin are wedded like Psyche to Eros, they will drift apart at the moment of death, which is the second or spiritual death. To "unveils the meaning of these words" is to understand the dyadic nature of our divine essence: the soul and her mystical companion, their bond, their purposes, and the roles they play in the ronde of infinite life. Neither faith nor deeds will buy us a seat in paradise, but a willful confluence of soul and *syzygos* will give birth to the **twy-formed god** rising immortal into the plenitude. That is the promise of the first Logion, and it will be fulfilled through the gnosis unlocked by the wisdom of Thomas. The greatest enigma in our existence is not the purpose of life but that of our death, and the wisdom of Thomas lie open before our eyes to help us crack the mystery.

Reigning over the Entirety - Logion 2

> *Jesus said: "He who seeks, let him not stop seeking until he finds. When he finds, he will be troubled; when he is troubled, he will be amazed and will reign over the entirety."*

Should the truth be reassuring, pleasing, comforting? Should it conform to what we expect, like, or want it to be? Must it be what we were raised to believe? Can it be found in the dominant or fringe paradigms of our society? If the salvific knowledge is to set us free from the world, it cannot speak of anything like unto the things of the world. Instead, it must break the shackles of the matter/mind, shatter the maze of our carnival mirrors, and awake us from our psycho-spiritual slumber, which can all be troubling indeed. The seeker, then, cannot be satisfied with the nebulous soup of contemporary pop-spirituality but must dedicate the totality of his existence to finding a gate out of the circle of life. There is not a single gate, but every single being has, hidden in his depths, the one key different from all the others to exit the conditional world and enter—not as a subject, but as a sovereign—the wonders of the entirety.

Within and without - Logion 3 (Part One)

> *Jesus said: "If your leaders tell you, 'behold, the kingdom is in the sky,' then the birds will precede you in the sky. If they tell you, 'It is in the sea,' then the fish will precede you. Instead, the mystical sovereignty (†) is within you and before your eye."*

The sea refers to the depths of our psyche, the "inside," and the "heaven" is a place "outside." By directing us singly to one or the other, the "leaders" use a strategy of telling half-truths to misguide us and force a split between the soul and her *syzygos*. That is so because the soul—the sum of our experiential and emotional memories—falls within the boundaries of our natural perception, whereas pneuma—the root and essence of all things—is the element "outside" of our natural perception. The mystical sovereignty is not a place where the swimming fishes, the flying birds, or the souls of the departed can go, but the **henosis** of the soul with her divine counterpart, who find each other when we understand the nature of the within and the without. Everything is pervaded by a psychic thrust, originator and sustainer, life and light, a supernal will or sempiternal **Desire** that focalizes within, becoming the consciousness and the mind that spawns the soul. In turn, the within and the without meld into a mirror for the soul. And the more the soul gazes at her reflection, the more it takes the shapes and substance of that for which she longs the most: a savior twin to love her with the passion out of which the paradise of the mystical sovereignty blossoms.

Our "leaders" have sided, unwittingly or not, with the **supersubstantial** entities called archons (see Appendix 2) in gnostic literature. The archons manipulate the **rulers**—our secular and religious administrators—in such a way that the designs of the leaders serve the aims of their masters. The survival of the archons depends on the continuation of the physical world, and their interest is in keeping our divine essence trapped in matter. The leaders solidify their elite status by means of a tight control of institutions and belief systems. Thus, we should expect those with authority among us to disseminate, reiterate, and support popular views and ideas that do not point to a path of liberation but to roundabouts that keep the divine essence bound to the material realm.

The surest way to find the mystical sovereignty is to be aware of its reaches both within and outside of us (see also Logion 77).

—

† I have elected to use "mystical sovereignty" in lieu of the traditional "kingdom." There is a widespread consensus that the kingdom promoted by Jesus in the

scriptures has nothing to do with physical boundaries and refers instead to a non-physical reign. Logion 2 clearly indicates that salvation leads to reigning over the entirety. "Mystical sovereignty" appears to me to describe better the promise of a transcendental state as understood by Thomas. However, I have preserved the word "kingdom" when used by the disciples. As we will see, the followers of Jesus who question him occasionally in the sayings did not appear to comprehend the mystical aspect of the kingdom and maintained instead the expectation of either a divine power on earth (e.g. Logion 113) or a place in heaven (e.g. logion 22).

The Knowledge of One's Self - Logion 3 (Part Two)

> *"When you know yourselves, then they will know you, and you will realize you are the sons of the father who lives. However, if you do not know yourselves, then you exist in poverty, and you are the poverty."*

We persistently hear our malaise and troubles in life are due to a lack of self-esteem, and that it has become imperative to rebuild our fragile, damaged sense of worth while helping our children develop a feeling of pride. However, all what we appear to develop is self-preoccupation at best, arrogance at worst. Our failure is in striving to esteem our natural self when we should learn instead to know the higher Self beyond the mind. When we surrender to the true, unclouded will of our *syzygos*, we arrive at an awareness of our origins and destiny as descendants of the god-being. If we do not receive this understanding or gnosis, then no material riches, worldly successes, talents, skills, or "inner beauty" can ever make up for our spiritual loss.

The Child of Life - Logion 4

> *Jesus said: "The older man will not hesitate to ask a child seven (†) days old about the place of life, and he will live. For many who are first will be last, [and] many of the last will be first, and they will become a* **monad** *(††)."*

It is doubtful an actual "child seven days old" could answer any metaphysical question except in the wonderland of religious scriptures where the miraculous is frequent. Logion 4 is telling us to seek wisdom from the child of life and light (the "inner child," to use a horrible, popular cliché), the nascent living eidolon nurtured by the soul to grow as her savior twin. The growth of the etherealized child is proportionate to the attention the soul is giving him. At last, when she embraces her eternal companion, the divine essence is freed from the physical universe and the soul is saved from her carnal prison.

Hippolytus of Rome left us the earliest surviving reference to a gospel of Thomas, in the which he makes mention of Logion 4:

> *[The Naassenes] speak...of a nature which is both hidden and revealed at the same time and which they call the thought-for kingdom of heaven which is in a human being. They transmit a tradition concerning this in the Gospel entitled "According to Thomas," which states expressly, "The one who seeks me will find me in children of seven years and older, for there, hidden in the fourteenth aeon, I am revealed.*

Note that the child in this quote is no longer seven days old but a seven-year-old (see Logion 21), and that the "thought-for-kingdom" (mystical sovereignty) is clearly described as an inner transformation (see Logion 3, part 1). Those who are first in the affairs of the world, though, may find themselves last to reach everlasting life because their mundane preoccupations keep them from nurturing their connection to the *syzygos* who can save them. They are absentee parents, so to speak, who will realize belatedly they have missed their chance to create an everlasting bond with their unique, etherealized child.

The child also symbolizes the beginning, "7" being the number of days in the biblical account of the creation. And it is by looking into the beginning—metaphorically questioning a seven-day-old child—that we can best understand the end, and our destiny (see Logion 18).

† "7" is not only the amount of days the **demiurge** needed to create the world and rest, but it is also the number of planets the ancients could distinguish as part of the cosmos. Thus, "7" is related to the realm of matter and by extension to the archons who are its rulers.

Hebraic sacred texts are full of those symbolic figures the significance of which need not concern us. There is a mystic in numbers, and "7" is a most mystical one: research shows that the majority of people asked to pick any number between 1 and 10 will choose "7."

†† There is much confusion among the translators and interpreters of the gospel of Thomas with regard to a recurring, key metaphysical concept variously translated as becoming "one and the same," "a single one," "a single thing," "one alone," or "solitary." For all these, I have substituted the word "monad" that better reflects the mystical, transcendental state described by Thomas.

The Mirror in the Depths - Logion 5

> *Jesus says: "Know that which is in your presence, and that which is veiled from you will be unveiled to you. Nothing veiled will not be unveiled; nothing buried [will not be unearthed]."*

As Jesus stands in front of the disciples, so does the living eidolon face us (see Preamble). And what is even closer to us that we do not see? Our soul! It is no small task to figure out our own nature and yet, humankind seems to skip this fundamental step to go in search of an elusive god they never find. Once we know the nature of the soul, we can fine-tune our inner sight to her mirror image reflected in the depths within. The reflection of the innermost is living: not only will it reveal that which was previously concealed, it will also take the shapes of a savior twin of the soul. Nothing stays hidden from those who recognize their dyadic nature and grow in intimacy with the divine being they evoke from within (see also Logion 70).

* * *

The myth of Narcissus is commonly interpreted as a parable for the perils of vanity, but its significance and relevance are better understood in the light of Logion 5.

Narcissus, whose beauty is unequaled, represents the soul. Seeing his figure reflected on the surface of a pond, he is enthralled. The tale is an allegory for the soul captivated by the eidolon reflected on the mirror of the depths. The soul does not fall in love with her image per se but is taken with the dweller in the innermost who has robed himself in that image (see Logion 15). Forgetting all earthly cares, she falls in the embrace of the beloved and dies to the physical world to be reborn symbolically as a delicate, perennial (suggesting a cycle; see Logion 18) in an incorruptible ethereality.

The Seeker's Ethics - Logion 6

His disciples asked him: "Do you want us to fast?" and "what is the way to pray?" "Should we make donations?" and "which foods should we avoid?" Jesus said: "Do not tell lies, and do not do what you abhor. For all that is witnessed by the heavens. Nothing veiled will not be unveiled; nothing covered will remain so."

The disciples are fully conditioned to follow the traditional devotions and rites of their time. In similar fashion, we are conditioned by the many protocols and observances, secular or religious, imposed on us since early childhood.

Rituals are effective means of thought manipulation, frequently used by religions, occult organization, and secret confraternities. Symbolically understood, elegant, sober liturgies have great aesthetic value and can elevate the soul to lofty heights, revealing wonders hitherto unknown. Alternatively, epoptic ecstasies, telestic rapture, and even sacred orgiastic practices can plunge the soul into the innermost from which she may emerge illumined and free from the constrictions that prevented the surrendering to her image in the depths. Unfortunately, most ritualized ceremonies have become ends in themselves, empty conventions that are more binding than they are liberating and no longer inspire. They are the spiritual smoke and mirrors produced by the hidden rulers of the cosmos and their minions to further their dominance over humanity under the pretense of setting the believer apart from the infidel. Religious customs and traditions are unnecessary distractions diverting us away from the true savior and into overzealous concerns and entanglements (see for instance Logion 53).

The dualist mystic can dispense with the ceremonious and the sanctimonious. With a simple ethos that does not need to agree with the rules and values of society, he rises above the world and avoids falling in the ritualistic traps of the rulers. The Druze—a syncretic, Abrahamic faith that incorporated elements of various philosophies, including Gnosticism, Neoplatonism, and Hinduism— could have been inspired by the same wisdom Thomas recorded:

> ... *they believe that rituals and ceremonies have caused Jews, Christians, and Muslims to turn aside from "pure faith". They argue that individuals who believe that God will forgive them if they fast and pray, will commit transgressions in the expectation of being forgiven - and then repeat their sins. The Druze thus eliminated all elements of ritual and ceremony; there is no fixed daily liturgy, no defined holy days, and no pilgrimage obligations. The Druze perform their spiritual reckoning with God at*

all times, and consequently need no special days of fasting or atonement.

—Source: jewishvirtuallibrary.org

* * *

We all tell lies. And the more complex the social frame is the more inevitable the lying gets. To disguise the truth is not always wrong or sinful per se because it happened to be a natural, psychological strategy that is often necessary. However, when we mislead and falsify to gain a personal advantage at the expense of others, duplicity turns into a way of life that mirrors the behavioral mechanisms of the archons who deceive and take advantage of humankind in order to ensure their own survival. Denial and self-deception too are tragic shades of lie that bring emotional suffering to the perpetrator. Such is the conclusion reached by the novelist and philosopher Fyodor Mikhailovich Dostoyevsky in his novel The Brothers Karamazov:

Above all, don't lie to yourself. The man who lies to himself and listens to his own lie comes to a point that he cannot distinguish the truth within him, or around him, and so loses all respect for himself and for others. And having no respect he ceases to love.

Deceit is the first step in seeking to impose a direction, a choice, or a condition on someone else. Significantly, we rarely want for ourselves what we attempt to force on fellow beings. Hence the exhortation of Thomas not to tell lies or do (unto others) that which we abhor (for ourselves). This is by far a more direct, reasonable, and practical proposition than the classical Christian, so-called Golden Rule, which can be a subtle weapon in the hands of those who yield the most influence (the establishment). Indeed, what one may find reasonable, just, or necessary is not as a matter of course that which another would choose for himself. Moral codes inevitably give legitimacy to the fanatics who seek to impose on entire populations that which they feel is best for them. This maneuver is typical of missionary efforts advanced by Muslims, Catholics, Mormons, Hindus, Buddhists, and Evangelists alike, and their zeal is a direct consequence of the Golden rule carried out to its logical ends. If everyone was following the sober, unassertive ethos of Thomas (akin to the Taoist's "action of non-doing," or *wu-wei*), there would be no need for manufactured moral compasses.

Wealthy industrial nations wish to see other countries follow—for their "own good"—their favorite political and economic systems and are not above forcing the hand of a reluctant people. But the good intentions turn into ill-thought policies and lack of foresight that pave the roads for unforeseen problems and misery. It is common for charitable acts to have disastrous corollaries, but the simple principles proposed by Thomas spare the honest soul many an embroilment and prevent well-intended meddling from making things more complicated for our neighbor.

The maze of deception into which we move was patterned after the original lie uttered to man by the "great architect of the universe":

> *But of the tree of the knowledge of good and evil, thou shalt not eat of it: for in the day that thou eatest thereof thou shalt surely die.*
>
> —Genesis 2:17

The events of Eden illustrate the shadowy dominion of the archons who promulgate rules and demands that dictate our thinking process and behaviors. Adam represents humankind, and the god who walked in the garden stands for the structure that governs the conditional world. Here are the lies of Eden:

- If Adam ate the fruit of the tree of knowledge, he would die. In truth, only the physical body perishes and decay; our essence is eternal and cannot die.
- If Adam obeyed God, he would remain forever blissful in the paradisiacal garden. But the bliss promised to Adam was that of ignorance, and the body of clay made for him was but a cage for his divine essence.
- God's motivations were Adam's wellbeing and happiness. In reality, the God who walked in the garden only had his own selfish interests at heart. Keeping Adam ignorant and captive as in a zoo, the demiurge could thrive on the emotional life of his prisoner.

Whether we are sold a pill to cure our ills, an elected representative to care for our ills, a system to prevent our ills, or a moral philosophy to make our ills acceptable, we can suspect ulterior motives with roots in the genesis of mankind. The Logia of Thomas are the antidote to the poisons that trickle into our minds. They reveal who crafted our chains and how to break them. We know they speak the truth because, unlike the false promises of those who hold power over our lives, they give us freely and unconditionally the means to become the instrument of our own salvation.

The Primordial Duality in Man - Logion 7

> *Jesus said: "Blessed is the lion who is consumed by the man and becomes man; cursed is the man who is consumed by the lion who becomes man."*

In the ancient world of Thomas, the lion was an emblem of royalty and represented divine sanction. References to lions in Judaism also emphasize their ferocity, signifying an antagonist force that needs to be overpowered. Obviously, the saying is allegorical. An esoteric symbolism of the beast here refers to the primordial, intrinsic duality of man who was formed (along with the whole of material creation) at the point of origin of two diffluent, opposite forces: a divine, psychic thrust on the one hand, and its opposite, entropic principle, the pull of stasis, on the other. Hence, the bewildering saying gets clearer when the lion is understood as the zoomorphic embodiment of a dual psychic tide at the origin of physical existence. That is how the "lion becomes man." When recognized, and properly channeled ("consumed," or absorbed), the numen that formed us becomes the wings of Eros that carry Psyche to her divine destiny. And that is why the lion is "blessed." A tide however always implies an ebbing of the flow: the waters that move beyond the main body and over the land also withdraw to the core (**Apeiron**). If the primal flow is left unrecognized and untamed, the soul loses the means of salvation, and the "cursed" man is drawn back ("consumed by the lion") toward annihilation. Man is ruled by his primeval, destructive instincts until he rises above the beast within. According to writer of esoterica Juan García Atienza, the rule of the Knight Templars prohibited them from hunting except in the case of lions, perhaps as a reminder of the words of the first apostle:

> *Be sober, be vigilant; because your adversary the devil, as a roaring lion, walketh about, seeking whom he may devour.*
>
> —1 Peter 5:8

The curious allegory of the lion and the human in Thomas also resurfaces as an archetype in the Tarot de Marseille. The card called "La Force" depicts a woman (the soul) subduing a lion: a worthy image of the soul's triumph over primordial animality, the victory of the psychic thrust over the pull of stasis.

* * *

Alternatively, the first verse of the Logion may refer to the way the flesh of dead animals, and its decay sustain biological life. This can be regarded as a blessing, even from a dualist standpoint, because out of this cycle of life in the material realm the human soul is born to be the instrument of liberation for the divine essence. The second verse speaks of the dire situation of the humans who do not develop a soul capable of seeing her reflection in the depths. Metaphorically, they are dominated, or consumed, by animality: earthy life is the beginning and the end for them because they are never saved from physicality and matter to become spiritually alive (see also Logion 11). They are directed and controlled by impulses instead of being guided by the living eidolon.

The Little Fish - Logion 8

> *And he said: "Man can be compared to a wise fisher who cast his net at sea and drew it up full of small fish from below (the surface). Among them the wise fisher found a fine large fish. He threw away the fry back into the sea, and he had no difficulty choosing the*

large fish. He who has an ear to lend, let him listen."

The first parable-like saying of Thomas breaks away from the author's cryptic, mystifying style and surprises us with its common sense thrust, and childlike simplicity. Indeed, the wisdom of the fisher resembles the practicality of the child who discards his smaller treats in favor of the biggest one. Many a logion in Thomas' gospel play on the esoteric theme of a return to childhood as the prerequisite for the liberation of the divine essence. If we are asked to lend an ear attentively, there must certainly be matters of foremost importance to be learned from the fisher who chose the large fish.

In the last paragraph of his massive epic novel *Musashi*, Eiji Yoshikawa gives the readers who for months had been kept enthralled by the characters' adventures (the novel was originally serialized), a surprising conclusion:

The little fishes, abandoning themselves to the waves, dance and sing, and play, but who knows the heart of the sea, a hundred feet down? Who knows its depth?

The philosophical wink is obvious: we the readers are the little fishes, always preoccupied by trifles and frivolities at the surface while incognizant of the great, meaningful depths were our essence dwells. That is also the key to the understanding of Logion 8.

Unlike his counterparts, the fishers of men in the Gospel of Matthew, the gnostic fisher of Thomas has no intention to turn the fry into a flock. His concern is with his own soul, the large fish from the inward abyss.

* * *

I like visiting public aquariums, and when I do, I am always haunted by the gaze of the enormous fish dawdling silently, peering through the glass at all those humans they may find very foolish. I often think they epitomize the old soul full of wisdom.

The Three Classes of Souls - Logion 9

> *Jesus said: "Behold, a sower came with a handful (of seeds) to sow. Some fell onto the road; the birds came to pick them. Others fell onto the rock, and neither could they take root, nor did they produce ears. Yet others fell among the thorns that choked them, and the worms ate them. Still others fell upon good soil and produced good fruits, yielding sixty per measure and a hundred and twenty per measure."*

Prior to the unearthing of the Gospel of Thomas, this saying was already known in the Gospel of Matthew as the Parable of the sower, a heavily edited allegory accompanied by a detailed interpretation of its symbolism. The clever editor of Matthew makes Jesus explain how the seeds spread by the sower represent the good news of the kingdom for the benefit of the persistent believers. In effect, the revision transforms the parable into a cautionary tale about the perils of not heeding the priests and preachers and neglecting to obey their holy writ to the letter. In Thomas however, the parable is presented without interpolation and enjoins the reader to discover his own answer to the riddle of the sower and the seeds.

The seeds are a common gnostic illustration for the heavenly parcels (or sparks) of pneuma fallen into matter. The parable does not highlight the need to listen to the words of God; it speaks of our essence reaching its destiny.

Once a cosmos is formed out of the two diffluent, opposite forces (see Logion 7), the psychic thrust spreads throughout the physical realm, triggering biological life and pushing forward until mind, consciousness, and the soul arise. When the reflection of the soul in the depths becomes her savior twin, the two can become a monad and give birth to a twy-formed god. Unfortunately, only a few of the initial seeds reach that loftier state of their journey.

The innermost of the *hylici*—those who cannot transcend the material world—never reflects their souls sufficiently. Figuratively, the divine seed in them is "picked" by the birds (overtaken by the pull of stasis, or "consumed by the lion," as we have seen in Logion 7) or left to dry and wither "onto the rock" (the matter).

The *psychici* strive to distance themselves from the grasp of physicality but fall prey to the distractions of religions, sects, or purveyors of spirituality (see Logion 6). They are choked by treacherous thorns and eaten by the worms who have crawled up their soul.

Only the *pneumatici*, those who breathe the divine breath, the chosen, recognize the living eidolon of their soul who blossoms into her savior twin. And from those two is born the twy-formed god. The seed has become a tree, then a fruit, and a flower at last.

* * *

The numerical formula at the end of the logion recalls the stages of maturity: 60 as the natural onset of old age, and 120 as the optimum number of years granted to men by the biblical creator. The seeds fallen on good soil are metaphorically the old souls, that is endowed with the greatest wisdom and breadth of experience.

The Burning Spirit - Logion 10

> *Jesus said: "I have cast the fire upon the world and, behold, I watch over until it blazes."*

This saying has three levels of meaning.

The "fire" is the divine **spirit**. That much we can infer from other sacred texts (see for instance Acts 2: 3-4 or Luke

3:16). This divine breath, or pneuma, subsequently actualizes in the physical plane as the psychic thrust that sustains organic existence, and a living presence, or *syzygos*, to guide the souls. In "the truthful heart" of the chosen, the *syzygos* becomes a living eidolon set ablaze by a desire to rise with the soul. Having taken over the core of our being, it matures into the savior twin who inflames a passion in the soul and burns through the flesh to set her free. Such is the course of the divine spirit watched over by the god-being who can see concurrently the beginning and the end.

A second level of understanding relates to the salvific knowledge that is troubling (see Logion 2). Such knowledge is esoteric, transmitted not through massive missionary efforts, but discreetly through receptive individuals. Alas, when gnosis transpires in the world, it is commonly regarded as a heretical danger and met with furious opposition likened to a blazing fire. Such was the case during the fanatical, violent campaigns of suppression the Church of Rome waged against pagans and gnostics. No sooner had the Christians recovered from being persecuted themselves that they became efficient, eager persecutors in turn. The infamous inquisition was initially created as a systematic tool to crush the spread of the Cathar faith and wipe it into oblivion, which was carried out successfully.

Lastly, divinity (the god-beings) is self-sustained through descent into physicality where the souls are born. The successive **tides of Apeiron** set the divine psychic thrust against the pull of stasis, creating an alchemical furnace that gives rise to the soul, her *syzygos*, and the twy-formed god issued from their confluence—the return to divinity.

From the Physical to the Transcendent - Logion 11

> *Jesus said: "This heaven and the one above it will pass; and those who are dead are not alive, and those who are alive will not die. In the days you ate that which is dead, you made it alive; when you are in the light, what will you do? On the day you were one, you made two. When you have become two, however, what will you do?"*

At first impression this saying may appear muddled, but upon examination we discover the Logion describes the passage from the physical realm to an etherealized state.

The *pneumatici*, who were spiritually alive through their temporal journey, will enter the mystical sovereignty and be sustained by uncreated light just like the earthly body is nourished by the decay of matter (†). Their souls will live in the everlasting dreams of the god-beings, free from the corruptibility of the cosmos.

The *psychic*i and the *hylici* are dead spiritually even as they walk among us. They cannot escape the confines of the conditional world, following the separation of the *syzygos* and the soul at the time of death, their dispersed memories will linger ghost-like throughout matter.

"On the day we were one," we were but a sempiternal Desire imprinted on the course of the divine psychic thrust that sustains and directs all life. Thenceforth, biological life flourished on Earth through the myriad of organisms that developed into sentient beings, becoming the medium for the rise of a soul in the humans and the animals capable of forming emotional reminiscences. In man, the psychic thrust splits, giving him his dyadic nature of soul and eidolon. What do we do when we become aware of our living image? That living eidolon responds to the expectations of the soul to become her savior twin; and when the soul embraces her twin, a twy-formed god is born anew.

—

† Even if one abstains from the flesh of dead animals, the decay and rotting of all things makes up the ground that produces aliments. And as soon as we remove our nutriment from its source, it oxidizes and spoils unless we can preserve it. Corruptibility literally nourishes us.

"Holder of the Heel" - Logion 12

> *The disciples asked Jesus: "We know that you will leave us. Who (then) will rule over us?" Jesus replied: "From your*

> *place you will go to James the Just for the sake of whom heaven and earth came into being."*

The historicity and identity of James the Just is a fascinating question from a scholarly perspective but of no import with regard to the liberation of our dyadic essence. The gospels, canonical or not, will always lead the literalist down the endlessly meandering paths of mythological tall tales, but the dualist mystic who seeks the salvific knowledge looks for an esoteric subtext in the scriptures. He is interested in meaning over the facts that concern the scholar and the academician.

"James" is etymologically *Ya'aqov* or "holder of the heel," referring to Jacob the son of Isaac who was born holding the heel of his twin Esau. James is likened to Jacob who "was made lord over" his twin brother (see Genesis 25:23 and 27:37). Thomas claims the very "heathen and earth came into being" for James. This unparalleled and mysterious pronouncement, befitting a god more than a mortal, shows the figurative nature of Logion 12. If Jacob was the twin and lord of Esau (who represents the soul as the earthiest of the two brothers), we must see "James," not as the historical figure he might have been (†), but as another metaphor for the savior twin of the soul. The writer of these veiled words is telling his audience they do not need a prophet to guide them. Once they understand the sayings, they will know "the Just," the living eidolon who is within them wherever they are (††). It is indeed for him that the physical world became a cradle; and to him who is the veritable savior the divine realm belongs.

—

† If indeed the logion were referring so approvingly to the historical James, it is impossible that Jesus would later denigrate the Jewish custom of circumcision (see Logion 53) which was most certainly revered by the leader of the faction of Christianity closest traditionally to Judaism. (See Galatians 2:11-12). It must also be noted that *to'am* (twin), the Hebrew transliteration of the Aramaic from which the name Thomas is derived, was not even a given name in the time of Jesus. Its use to designate a specific individual as "the twin" is yet another indication the gospels, canonical or apocryphal, are not historical but allegorical.

†† Note that the disciples are told to go from "their place" to where James the Just is. This can be interpreted as a metaphor for removing oneself from the world (see Logion 56) and look within where the living eidolon has his place.

The Secret Knowledge of Thomas - Logion 13

> *Jesus told his disciples: "Compare me and tell me whom I resemble." Simon Peter told him: "You are like a just angel." Matthew told him: "You are*

> *like a wise philosopher." Thomas told him: "Master, I do not have words to say whom you resemble." Jesus replied: "I am not your master. Because you have drunk, you are intoxicated from the bubbling spring I measured." And he took him aside and told him three words. When Thomas returned to his companions, they asked him: "What did Jesus say to you?" Thomas told them: "Should I tell you one of the words he told me, you would take stones to fling at me, and fire would come out of the stones to burn you."*

Readers who subscribe to the notion of a historical Jesus regard him either as a supernatural being or as a sage. Similarly in Thomas—while the doctrines of the son of God, redeemer-savior had yet to be invented—the disciples see their teacher as "a just angel" or "a wise philosopher." However, Logion 13 subtly points to the allegorical nature of Jesus: Thomas is unable to describe his teacher because that teacher is the living eidolon or holy presence within. In this saying, a literal Jesus withdraws ("I'm not your teacher") behind the veritable source of the revelations from which Thomas received his inspiration. Thomas has drunk from the fount, the "bubbling spring," and is now "intoxicated" with the lofty gnosis he will preserve for the benefit of future generations.

Jesus takes Thomas aside and tells him three words that the other disciples will not be told. This corresponds to the living eidolon revealing three things to the soul. The number 3 hints at the triadic motif of the soul, the *syzygos*, and the twy-formed god risen from a henosis of the two parents. The radical idea that the divine is an indwelling triad would have been an anathema to the Jews, and, should had they been taught such thing, they would have reacted with violence (see also Logion 10). Yet, the unified essence that ultimately transforms in a polymorphous triad permeates all matter, including stones (see Logion 77), and can purify the soul, enflame the heart, or devastate the mind like the fire of the Light-Bringer.

* * *

Secrecy has always appealed to the human psyche and is frequently linked to the notion of power. The idea is that those who are in power know secrets, and those who know secrets acquire power. This rhetoric is found everywhere nowadays from "conspiracy theories" to dubious empowering techniques such as the so-called "Law of attraction." Unsurprisingly, there is also no shortage of books that includes the words "secret" and/or "power" in hackneyed tittles, promising the readers they can access sources of knowledge others do not have and gain privileges and influence in the world.

In the gospel of Thomas, the dynamics of secrecy and power are in evidence as well but for an entirely different purpose. Thomas' thinking is that true power can only be over oneself and derived from the gnosis within. This sacred wisdom is veiled rather than occult and kept secret inasmuch as it must be protected from the misunderstandings and profane interests that stem from vulgarization.

The Pneumatici - Logion 14

> Jesus told them: "If you fast, you will beget a sin for yourselves; and if you pray, you will be condemned; and if you give alms, you will damage your spirits (†). And, should you go into a land and walk the districts, if you are received, eat that which is set before you (and) heal the sick among them. It is not that which you will eat that will defile you, but that which comes out of your mouth."

The only matter of concern for the *pneumatici* is the veritable knowledge that saves. They do not have to separate themselves artificially from the world or look the part of the pious and the devout. The codified rituals, observances, rules, and moral conduct (see Logion 6) imposed by the religions of the world on the faithful are a poison to the mind and the rulers' instruments to shackle the soul and atrophy the savior twin. The mark of the *pneumatici* is caution with words and actions that grow from the dictates of the heart. There is no other demand placed on the soul than to be true to the unclouded, mystical Desire within. Nothing can defile the flesh because it belongs to the world of matter and decay and is already defiled. But our souls can be defiled by the rationales we promote and to which we adhere. The sickness the *pneumatici* can heal is ignorance and malnourishment of a soul deprived from a deeply rooted connection with her *syzygos* (see Logion 40).

—

† The word "spirit" is sparsely used (Logia 14, 29, 44, 53, and 114) in Thomas vocabulary, and always refers to a living, immaterial entity. In that same sense it is employed in John 4: 24 (see Logion 15 below) and in the anecdote from *Pistis Sophia* quoted under Logion 22. In Logion 14, the plural form clearly indicate something countable—that can be thought as many—in this case, the savior twin of each soul. The plural "spirits" as in good or high spirits is a modern usage.

The Self Triumphant - Logion 15

Jesus said: "When you look upon him who was not born of the woman,

> *prostrate yourselves on your faces and worship him: that one is your father."*

The "father" is not born of a woman and appears as a "person." Who is this mysterious birth-less, anthropomorphic figure worthy of worship?

"**I AM**," the hypostasis of consciousness is self-sustained: Desire carried through a psychic thrust and manifested on the physical plane as the **dyad** of soul and eidolon, which in turn gives rise to the twy-formed god eternally renewed through his projection into matter. The "father," then, is the highest expression of that cycle without beginning or end, originator of all things, but also, in his various aspect, parent, brother, lover, and god of the soul. (See also Logia 18 and 29)

The Apostle John wrote that "God is a spirit" (see John 4:24 KJV). He cannot be "born of a woman." His manifestation occurs through a circular series of transcendental metamorphoses:

- Desire is carried forth upon the divine breath (pneuma), which stirs the **field of Apeiron**. With each exhalation, the "I AM" dreams, and a new plane of existence begins. All the realms thus created are penetrated by the god's psychic thrust that sustains and nourishes life until consciousness, awareness, self-awareness, and finally the soul (the anamnesis) arise within sentient beings.

- A *syzygos* grows and strengthens in the human beings whose souls become aware of her living image within.
- When the soul embraces her reflection in the innermost, the *syzygos* becomes the savior twin, betrothed and savior of the soul.
- In mutual embrace, the savior and the saved can give birth to the twy-formed god, which is the inhalation of the "I AM" who breathes eternally over the field of Apeiron.

Thus is completed the cycle of reality. Thus is "I AM" the invisible father of the human race, and the god-being we should worship.

* * *

Paradoxically, "I AM" is both the son and father of the soul. To find out the truth about ourselves, the gospel of Thomas forces us to abandon the linear thinking that makes us apprehend reality as an unfurling chain of cause and effect from past to present. Reality instead is a loop wherein all that could possibly be already is. Our perception of states and events at any moment depends on the particular window from which we are looking into the whole.

Divide and Conquer - Logion 16

> *Jesus said: "Men may be thinking that I came to cast peace upon the world,*

and they do not know I came to cast divisions upon the earth: fire, sword, war. Out of the five in a house, three will come to be opposed to two and two opposed to three, the father opposed to son, and the son opposed to the father, and they will stand upright—they being monads."

This is one of the few sayings from Thomas with a counterpart in the New Testament (see Luke 12:49-53).

Logia 10 and 13 warned us that esoteric knowledge let loose in the world would wreak havoc before it could elicit even a small measure of peace and harmony (†). Few are inclined to embrace a hidden knowledge likened to an all-consuming fire and a sword that "cast divisions" on Earth. Logion 16 explains that the war and disturbance the revelation of gnosis creates are more than religious dissensions and strife; they also happen within the hearts and minds of man.

Humankind, and the cosmos are the stage of a terrible clash between opposite impulses: the **tide of Apeiron** against the ebbing force of entropy; the *syzygos* against the mind; the savior twin who has a claim on the soul against the rulers who seek to keep us entrapped in matter. Man is divided under his own roof and a threat to himself because of the forces emanating from his multidimensional nature. The "house" is not one of stone, wood and cement, but the body of flesh in which the metaphysical crisis unfolds.

The contentions of Thomas must have baffled the redactor-copyists who worked with disparate sayings and stories (and a good deal of imagination) to compile the many "Gospels" circulated at the beginning of the Common Era. Editors interpreted Logion 16 as a prophecy of internecine feuds elicited by the word of God. Hence, we find in Luke 12:53 a family drama that involves not only father and son, but also mother, daughter, and (of course) mother in law. The second half of the saying can be understood either literally (as the author of Luke did) or figuratively.

If actual members of a household are in strong disagreement over religious matters, they may break family ties. However, if father and son (child) are respectively the underlying consciousness and the soul (see Logion 15 above) the two will ascend as a monad. When the father (in the form of the living eidolon) and the daughter/son (the soul) are united, they give rise to the third, holy being. Accounted together, they are the three in the house. As long as the soul fails to seek her living eidolon, she remains "opposed" to her father. Father and child estranged from each other defer the birth of the twy-formed god. Thus are the two "opposed" to the three. When the providential circumstances arise, however, divisions crumbles and the two meld into the third as poetically described in the cryptic, gnostic text *Pistis Sophia*:

> *That mystery knoweth why the twin-saviours have arisen and why the three Amēns have arisen. [...] And that mystery knoweth why the Mixture which existeth not, hath arisen and why it is purified.*

The "twin-saviors" are the living eidolon and the soul become saviors unto each other through the mutual passion that leads to their reciprocal liberation. They are twins because it is the reflection of the soul in the depths, the living eidolon, that takes the shape of her savior. The "three Amēns" constitute the holy triad of Soul, *syzygos*, and the holy child (the twy-formed god) born of their union (the "Mixture"). But the ends of this hallowed design are not met without considerable struggle and resistance. The processes of etherealization ("purification") engender conflictual dynamics ("father opposed to son and son opposed to father") deep in the psyche of the *pneumatici* who must abandon the preponderance of the mind and accept the authority of the father ("I AM") over the soul. They will not ascend as a monad unless the soul (daughter/son) severs her natural attachment to the mind dependent on physicality and loses herself in the embrace of the father.

* * *

The esoteric meaning of Logion 16 is echoed in Paul's letter to the Hebrews:

> *For the word of God is quick, and powerful, and sharper than any two-edged sword, piercing even to the dividing asunder of soul and spirit.*
>
> —Hebrews 4: 12

The word of god is compared to a sword that divides the soul and the *syzygos*. That is the salvific knowledge eliciting strife for the souls unable to abandon the world, including man-made religions and rationales. Divisions also appear between the *psychici* who seek redemption for their soul through an external savior and the agency of the church, and the *pneumatici* who seek liberation in the love of the soul for her divine image. Spanish writer of esoterica Juan García Atienza summarizes the mystagogic intent of Jesus' controversial pronouncements:

> *When he proclaims that he has not come to this world to bring peace, or when he suggests the necessity of breaking with romantic and family ties, he preaches not war or hate, but rather the necessity that human affections be channeled to the Divinity through primordial love.*
>
> —Juan García Atienza, *The Knights Templar in the Golden Age of Spain*

—

† Indeed, since its publication the Gospel of Thomas, far from bridging gaps, has reinforced entrenched opinions in opposed camps of religious orthodoxy. Had the manuscript been discovered a few centuries earlier, it would have

been branded as heretical and burnt along the individuals who read it.

Gnosis - Logion 17

> *Jesus said: "I will give you that upon which no eye has looked, and that which no ear has heard, and that which no hand has touched and did not occur to man's mind (alt. 'did not rise in man's heart')."*

The keys to unlocking the esoteric mysteries of the gospel of Thomas are:

- an awareness of the Soul-Eidolon dyadic nature of our essence
- an understanding of the dynamic and mutable eternal triad of Soul, *syzygos*, and the twy-formed god born of their union
- a comprehension of the principles of oneness, division, reunion, henosis, and begetting that underlie reality.

The intent of the salvific knowledge Thomas wrote down is to be the catalyst for a psychic conflict (see Logion 16 above), the resolution of which facilitates the manifestation of the living eidolon in the heart of man. The gnosis that subsequently takes hold of the mind of the *pneumatici* is not comparable to the philosophical and religious creeds with which we are already familiar. The next Logion will show us an instance of that which has never been seen, heard, touched or thought.

The Circular Nature of Reality - Logion 18

> *The disciples asked Jesus: "Tell us (about) our end: in what way will it come to be?" Jesus replied: "Have you unveiled the beginning so that you will be seeking after the end? For in the same place where the beginning is, the end will be. Blessed is he who will stand upright at the beginning; he will know the end, and he will not taste death."*

Why is there something rather than nothing? If God created us, who created God? Before the birth of the universe, was there a creator all alone and self-existing? Those are some of the most baffling questions that continue to occupy the thoughts of philosophers and mystics alike. But the *psychici*, such as the disciples who figure in Thomas' narrative, have a single, persistent, pragmatic concern in mind: they want to solve the enigma of death. Indeed, one of the strangest facts of existence is that nature built an organism designed to last forever, only to rig it with a self-destructing mechanism. In answer, Logion 18 gives them the keys to unlock the mystery of the circular and reflective qualities of reality.

When the soul elopes with her savior twin, the twy-formed god born of their henosis ignites from his own nature the spark sent on a course, through innumerable cycles, to become himself anew, the god-at the origin of the cycle. We are because we imagine ourselves into existence. We stand at the beginning and the end as the "I AM." We do not know death because we live eternally, but with a different level of awareness—a distinct angle of view—at each point of the circle that is the whole of consciousness and reality. Our life, as is, has already happened and is continually happening just as the countless other courses of life that fulfill the near-infinite potentialities of the tides of Apeiron. To stand blessedly at the beginning is to look through the eyes of a god-being. There never was a genesis per se, or a creation "ex nihilo," because everything that can be is; only, we are looking at it from one of many windows. Once the curtain of ignorance is lifted from the stage of reality, we will discover we are both the audience and the actors.

The Trees in Paradise - Logion 19

> *Jesus said: "Blessed is he who comes from the beginning before coming into being. If you are to become my disciples and listen to my words, these stones will become your servants. There are five trees in paradise that do not*

change (from) summer (to) winter, and their leaves do not fall. He who will know them will not taste death."

From Logion 18 we learned that the "one who comes from the beginning before coming into being" is the god-being perpetuating himself through us: the "I AM" we will become who was before we were; the eternally blessed child of Soul and Eidolon. When we heed gnosis, we liberate ourselves from the stones—which represent the physical world that is our prison—and matter is no longer the master but the servant, the medium that makes possible the perpetual rebirth of the twy-formed god.

What the five trees of Paradise might be, no one knows. The book of Genesis tells us about two trees planted in the middle of Eden: the tree bearing fruits of knowledge, and the tree of life. Adam was forbidden to eat of the former and was barred from the latter. We can infer the three other trees not specified in the myth of Eden bore fruits of vital importance as well. Indeed, the promise made by Thomas at the very beginning of his gospel (see Logion 1) is the same as in Logion 19: he who knows the trees (understands the esoteric meaning of the logia) will not know death. To unlock the revelations of the gospel of Thomas is to receive the keys of paradise and eat of all the trees therein.

* * *

Logion 16 mentioned five members in a household. Could there be a correlation between the five in the house and the five (trees) in paradise? We can imagine the five trees as: the knowledge of good and evil; the knowledge of the soul; the knowledge of the savior twin; the knowledge of the twy-formed god; the knowledge of eternal life. The first two pertain to physicality, the others to a transcendent realm. Each of them ensues from the one before, and the gift of everlasting life results from the totality of this gnosis. We can turn anew to *Pistis Sophia* where the "five trees" resurface to find echoes of this idea:

> *That mystery knoweth why the twin-saviours* [the soul and the savior twin] *have arisen and why the three Amēns* [soul, savior twin, twy-formed god] *have arisen.*
>
> *And that mystery knoweth why the five Trees have arisen and why the seven Amēns have arisen.*
>
> *And that mystery knoweth why the Mixture* [the confluence of the soul and the savior twin, or monad] *which existeth not, hath arisen and why it is purified* [released from matter].

The Nature of Eternal Life - Logion 20

The disciples asked Jesus: "Tell us, to what the kingdom of heaven can be compared?" He replied: "It can be compared to a mustard seed, smallest among all the seeds. However, when it falls on tilled ground, it sends out a large branch and becomes a shelter (for) the birds of the sky."

This Logion is the first in a series of similes used by Thomas to facilitate the understanding of complex principles while keeping them veiled to the *hylici* who do not apply their mind and heart to an understanding of the Ethereality.

To understand the nature of eternal life, the disciples ask to what the kingdom of heaven (†) can be compared. In esoteric language, "seeds" and "birds" are symbols for the parcels of pneuma and for the souls, respectively. Pneuma is "seeded" in the physical world and ushers biological evolution through its psychic thrust until the soul appears in sentient beings. Etherealization is the reward at the end of a journey from pneuma to soul, to the savior twin, to the rise of the twy-formed god.

The mystical sovereignty is not a locality in heaven but a transcendent, ecstatic state of soul and *syzygos* conjoined outside physicality. Pneuma grows from seed to tree, the **Pleroma** that shelters the souls (the birds of heaven) forever.

—

† Despite Jesus' best efforts to clarify its significance (see Logion 3), the disciples continue to regard the mystical

sovereignty as either a place in the heavens or a power coming from the sky.

The Enemies of the Soul - Logion 21

> *Mary told Jesus: "Whom do your disciples resemble?" He replied: "They resemble small children dwelling in a field that is not theirs. When the lords of the field come, they will say: 'Give us our field back.' To give it back to them, they strip naked in their presence and let them have their field. Therefore, thus I speak: Should the lord of the house realize the thief is coming, he would keep watch before he comes and would not permit him to tunnel into his house of his domain to take his goods. You, then, keep watch from the beginning of the world, gird your loins with great power lest the thieves find a way to come up to you; for the help you seek from the outside, they will find. Let there be in your midst a man of understanding. When the fruit split, he came quickly, sickle in hand, to reap it.*

He who has an ear to lend, let him listen."

Mary's question is not about the nature of discipleship: she wants to know the transformation of heart and mind that occurs in those who follow their *syzygos*. The answer comes in a highly elaborated allegory in which the soul and the *syzygos* are children (†) whose clothing represents the envelope of flesh. The context shows it is through the very act of "striping naked" that the children are able to give back the "field." All goes well for the souls who willingly rid themselves of their physical body and stand naked, in their pure state, to be embraced by their twin companion (see Logion 22). They renounce the material world—the field— that belongs to the archons, the supersubstantial entities who rule over the realm of matter.

The Logion continues with a warning to the owner of "the house," the *hylici*, who regard the body as the natural home of their consciousness and take the planet(s) for their domain. The archons (the thieves) are after the house's most valuable possession: the soul whom they need to keep captive on the physical plane in order to ensure the continuation of their own existence. This is the real death, the spiritual death that awaits those who are not metaphysically aware; a severing of the soul from the transcendental realm that could be hers. The "house" is the great battleground not for evil against good (which are never causal, but incidental), but between material and suprasensible forces. The price is the soul.

The last part of the Logion is an admonition to the *psychici* who fear for their soul but have yet to heed the true salvific knowledge. The "help" they seek is external, bound to religious organizations and dogmatic teachers. None of that is of any use against a powerful enemy who has long ago wormed its way into religion. The souls of the *psychici* too will remain trapped in the physical sphere unless they become a "man of understanding" and recognize where the "fruit is split": our inherent diadicity that is the crux of divinity.

Men of the world may scoff at the idea of parasitic, supersubstantial creatures coveting our memories. Yet, the fingerprints of the archons can be detected in the greatest danger facing us in our time: the rise of transhumanism and our unconditional surrender to the technology that serves the cloaked designs of our enemies. Virtual reality is already rewiring our brains to adapt to a new, fabricated universe within the created universe while disengaging our faculty to apprehend the natural world. Trapped in a prison within a prison, our inability to escape the world of materiality will be all but ensured. In the nightmarish visions they pass for a path to liberation, the prophets of the singularity want to upload human consciousness. Transformed into electronic bits, the souls of the posthumans would be captured in machines and cut off from the *syzygos* to face an uncertain fate worse than roaming the corridors of the house of Hades.

No wonder the "man of understanding" is likened to a reaper who hurries and give his soul away to her eternal companion, thus finding release from the clutches of the material world.

—

† Historically, children are a recurring image representing the soul and/or the spirit in religious texts, in literature, and in art. In his "Red Book," the famed founder of analytical psychology Carl Jung states:

> *I had to recognize and accept that my soul is a child and that my God in my soul is a child.*

The Savior twin - Logion 22

> *Jesus looked on little ones taking milk. He told his disciples: "These little ones taking milk can be compared to those who enter the mystical sovereignty." They asked him: "Will we enter the kingdom as little ones, then?" Jesus replied: "When you make the two a monad, the inside like the outside and the outside like the inside, and the above like the below, making the male and the female that monad so that the*

> *male will not be male nor the female female; when you make eyes in the place of an eye, and a hand in the place of a hand, and a foot in the place of a foot, an image in the place of an image, then you will enter [the mystical sovereignty]."*

In Logion 22 we find again the motif of childhood in a vivid picture that depicts the transformation one must undergo at the threshold of the mystical sovereignty. But it is not a simple matter of a return to innocence (accepting Jesus, as the neo-Christian may think) or of obeying godly laws (as a Mormon would reply); the soul will not rest in blissful eternity until she finds her own vehicle to immortality.

"These little ones taking milk" tell us something consequential about our soul: she is dependent and cannot stand on her own. Memories make up the soul and form a locus of individuality for as long as they are attached to either our mind or the *syzygos*. Our mind keeps the soul entrapped in the material world; the *syzygos* takes her in the beyond. When "the two are made a monad," the memories of the chosen are sealed to their legitimate, eternal heir. The divine essence made whole is the unique being—a twy-formed god—born of the coalescence of the soul and her savior twin released from the grip of matter.

The esoteric attributes of *syzygos* are:

- the "inside"—originating in and emerging from the depths
- the "above"—higher, suprasensible, heavenly
- the "male"—father (see Logion 15), active, the seed of divinity dispersed in matter, the projection of the "I AM" into physicality.

Those of Soul are:

- the "outside"—memories that constitute the soul come from our experience in and of the world
- the "below"—bound to the material sphere
- the "female"—mother (see Logia 79 and 105), passive, receptive, the recipient of the "I AM" in physicality.

Thomas describes the symbiosis of *syzygos* and Soul, who must grow alike, merging their attributes to coalesce into a whole. In the most cryptic part of the saying he illustrates the transcendental exit of the soul out of this world. The decaying body of flesh and bones that was her host and garment must be replaced by an etherealized body of light. Thus, an etherealized eye, hand, and foot are substituted for the physical eye, hand, and foot. A luciform counterpart to the carnal body is manifested as the soul's *syzygos*, a savior twin to draw her in his embrace.

Myths such as the abduction of Ganymede (†) by Zeus or the eloping of Eros with Psyche depict the mystical encounter of "he who lives" (the beloved) with the soul (the lover). Again, we find a confirmation of the allegory in

Pistis Sophia, which use the striking imagery of an anecdote involving Jesus as a child, and his "Spirit" twin:

> *When you were small, ... the Spirit came from on high and came to me, in my house, <u>looking like you</u>, and I did not recognize him, and <u>I thought it was you</u>. And the Spirit said to me, "Where is Jesus my brother, that I may meet him?" ... you were glad and said: "Where is he that I may see him? For I await him in this place." ... And we looked at you and at him, and found that <u>you resembled him</u>. And when he ... was freed, he embraced you and kissed you, and you kissed him, and <u>you both became one</u>.*

(Emphases are mine.)

In this miraculous event, Jesus is the prototype of the human beings on a journey of awakening, self-discovery, liberation, and etherealization. He is "the son of the god" as we are because the soul—the marker of our individuality—was born through the unfolding of the divine psychic thrust from its source in the god-being. In the passage above, Mary is witnessing the savior twin who reveals himself to her son Jesus. The two children become one to enter the plenitude of the mystical sovereignty.

* * *

The children represent the *syzygos* and the soul who share the "pure" attributes of childhood that are lost in adulthood: for the *syzygos*, vigor, potential, imagination, creativity, and a drive to be free; for the soul, curiosity, spontaneity, receptivity, and malleability. This notion did not escape Romanian sculptor Constantin Brâncuși who reportedly once claimed: "When we are no longer children, we are already dead." Beyond the obvious reference to the loss of child-like creative imagination, Brâncuși's words have a momentous, more literal significance: unless we re-create a child within, salvation will elude us, and we will be met not just with the death of the body in its time, but with spiritual death as well (see Logion 70). That is also the idea behind Jesus' famous statement:

> *Verily I say unto you, Except ye ... become as little children, ye shall not enter into the kingdom of heaven.*
>
> —Matthew 18:3

—

† In antiquity, Xenophon indicated the Ganymede myth was a telestic narrative, explaining that Zeus did not love not the shepherd boy, but his soul (his psychē).

The Chosen - Logion 23

> *Jesus said: "I will choose you, one out of a thousand and two out of ten thousand, and they will stand upright, being made a monad."*

To be "made a monad" is to have one's soul wedded to her savior twin (see also Logion 16). Sadly, only a few, the *pneumatici*, are willing to surrender their soul to her legitimate heir. They are the chosen, the "truthful and believing hearts," in whom the living eidolon has a dwelling place. They heed the call of the innermost until the spark of godhood is liberated from the cycles of life, and the soul is released from her carnal envelope. The chosen are not an elite arbitrarily plucked out of mankind by a paternalistic god, but the blessed of a time cycle in whom the sempiternal Desire overpowers at last the entropic pull of stasis.

Embedded in the saying is the "one-two-one" sequence, Thomas' recurring motif of oneness giving way to the psychic trust, and of duality followed by (re)union: from one proceed two, and the two unite as one.

The Light and the Darkness - Logion 24

> *His disciples asked: "Show us the place where you are because we need to seek it." He replied: "He who has an ear to lend, let him listen. Light exists within a man of light, and he becomes light to the entire world. If he does not become light, he is (alt. "there is") darkness."*

If their teacher was an actual person, no disciple would need to look for the place "where he is." We determined however that the Jesus of the logia is the god within (see Preamble), and we need to search our innermost for the hidden place where he has made his dwelling.

The "man of light" within whom light exists is the chosen (see Logion 23) who harbors the body of light which must be the next vehicle of the soul (see Logion 22). The disciples seek a savior outside themselves, but the only savior of the soul is the luminous angel who carries the divine light in us. The *pneumatici* who belong to that light (see Logion 50) illumine the whole world because they are the conduits for the divine light in the world and the instruments to repeal the darkness of chaos. Incidentally, one should always be wary of external light manifestations such as that witnessed accompanying religious and supernatural apparitions (including UFOs related events). The uncorrupted, uncreated light experienced by the dualist mystic is always within (internal) because all things perceived in the sensible world is corrupted by matter.

* * *

We perceive a conflict between light and darkness because the two coexist relatively to each other. Darkness is rest, passive, receptive. Light is movement, active, creative. The darkness can never overwhelm the light, only fill the place where it ceases to be. The light can never replace the darkness, only push it back. The association of darkness and light with evil and good in popular consciousness is misleading. Good and evil are not active, actual forces, but abstractions and perceptions that result from the tides of Apeiron with their opposite pulls.

Who Is Our Brother? - Logion 25

> *Jesus said: "Love your brother like your soul; guard him like the pupil of your eye."*

This saying has such a pragmatic and obvious moral implication, it is hard to see how its meaning could be anything but literal. Christianity constructed an entire ethical system around universal love of neighbors (Luke 10:27:37) and enemies alike (Matthew 5:45). There is however something fundamentally flawed and perverse about a moralistic code that requires to turn the other cheek (Matthew 5:38-40). Is a child starved in a concentration camp obliged to love his tormentors? Should we expect the 12th century Cathars who were subjected to the most horrific tortures under the supervision of the Dominicans friars to have kissed the hand of their torturers? In the Christian canon, Mark implies a step away from unconditional love toward a more restrictive view in the which our brother is "whoever does God's will" (see Mark 3:35). But who is the brother we must love and protect as we love and protect our own soul?"

The answer is found in a line of the *Pistis Sophia* (previously quoted with Logion 22): "Where is Jesus my brother, that I may meet him?" asked a mysterious spirit descended from on high, looking like the spitting image of Jesus. The boy Jesus in the *Pistis Sophia* acts as the prototype of the human soul, and the spirit is his savior twin brother. This is consistent with the idea of a figurative, transcendent family (as opposed to the literal, earthly one; see logia 55 and 101) in Thomas. The allegory of the *Pistis Sophia* mirrors that of the gospel of Thomas where the roles are reversed: Thomas represents the soul, and his twin brother is Jesus who stands for the living eidolon within (Logion 0). Our brother then, is no other than our own savior twin. That is the reason it is crucial to love and protect him by surrendering to his will and designs.

The Numinous Insight - Logion 26

> *Jesus said: "You see the mote in your brother's eye, yet you do not see the beam in your eye. When you cast the beam out of your eye, then you will be able to see to cast the mote out of your brother's eye."*

Logia 22, 25 and 26 all refer to the eye but with a notable progression from speaking of the physical organ to introducing the concept of a numinous insight, that is the capacity to apprehend nonphysical realities.

In the New Testament there is an emended version of this saying, which appears as an exhortation to self-awareness and a warning that one would be well advised to spend time in self-appraisal before undertaking to judge the character of others. (See Matthew 7:3-5) Although that "improved" allegory is now a celebrated adage, it masks the esoteric import of the original words of Thomas.

To notice a speck in someone's eye and trying to remove it is certainly an act of kindness. Wouldn't we do it to help a child? Isn't it remarkable that in Logion 25 the *pneumatici* are exhorted to "guard their brother like the pupil of one's eye?" This "brother," we found, is the savior twin of the soul, clothed in a body of light. To get the speck out of our brother's eye, then, is a metaphor for the care and attention we need to lavish on the savior twin of our soul. Yet, this cannot be done without first removing the beam from our own eye, which means overcoming the obstacles of physicality. And once we subdue our impulses to rely on the judgement of the mind—that which we perceive with "our own eyes"—we open ourselves to a numinous insight and begin to see reality through the pellucid eyes of our heavenly brother.

Sight and mind are indissociable. What we "see" exists only in our brains. So is the numinous insight associated with the "mind" of the *syzygos*.

Binding the Soul to the Transcendent Realm - Logion 27

> *"If you do not fast from the world, you will not find the mystical sovereignty. If you do not make the Sabbath a (true)*

> *Sabbath, you will not behold the father."*

The true Sabbath is not about abstaining from work or arguing endlessly over what may be permissible to do on one particular day of the week. The literalists and strict adherents to the creeds of the world concern themselves with an array of rites, conduct, codes and rules, losing sight of the veritable intent of religion to "bind" (from the Latin *religare*) the soul to the divine. To "fast from the world" and to make the "Sabbath a (true) Sabbath" is to be detached from earthly preoccupations, including religiously prescribed behaviors or actions. To distance oneself from worldly concerns, inasmuch as it is feasible, is to weaken the chains that tether our soul to matter while strengthening our ties to the living eidolon.

Once we rid ourselves of emotional involvement in the affairs of material existence, the life of our soul takes precedence until her apotheosis is reached and she sees the "father" in the countenance of the savior twin (Logion 15).

Standing Sober in the World - Logion 28

> *Jesus said: "I stood upright in the midst of the world and I appeared visibly to them in flesh; I found them drunk; I did not find any of them thirsting, and my soul grieved over the*

> *sons of men; for men are blind in their heart (alt. 'in their mind'), and they do not see; for they came to the world empty, (and) empty too they seek to leave the world. Meanwhile, they are drunk; when they sober from their wine, then they will repent."*

The revealer came into our flesh as the *syzygos*, and he does not have much of an audience: few of the children of men recognize the living eidolon of their soul within and thirst for its guidance. Humankind is drunk with the precepts of men and man-made religions. Their mind is blind, bereft of numinous insight. They come into the world empty because the soul does not appear until our first emotional memory is formed in the brain; they will leave empty because the living eidolon makes his abode in the heart of the truthful only. When the flesh had returned to the dust, the soul without her savior twin will remain forlorn and dream-like, drifting on the physical plane, seeking to attach herself to the familiar.

Just as we can remove "the beam" that hampers numinous insight (see Logion 26), we can sober up from the wine of meandering rationales that clouds our mind and drink of the living water that would quench our thirst forever (see Logion 74 as well as John 4:10-14). Thomas here uses the metaphor of drunkenness for humanity's willful ignorance of the ethereality in contrast to the imagery of a desirable intoxication brought about by the "bubbling spring" of "living water" (see Logia 13).

The Metamorphoses of Spirit - Logion 29

> Jesus said: "If the flesh comes into being because of spirit, it is a wonder; if, however, spirit (comes into being) because of the body, it is a greater wonder. Regardless, I am myself amazed how [this] great richness was placed in this poverty."

"Spirit" is a term that regrettably means little because it stands for almost anything conceivable that isn't physical. We do not have the adequate vocabulary to describe the myriad shades of the ethereality lying behind and beyond that which our senses allow us to gauge. This language gap hinders our understanding of the supersubstantial dimension and the transcendent realm.

When Thomas speaks of "spirit" twice in this logion, he uses the same sort of nuance as John (or at least his translators) who exclaims: "God is a Spirit, and they that worship him must worship him in spirit and in truth" (John 4: 24). The spirit that causes the flesh to come into existence is pneuma in its aspect of the divine psychic thrust (likened to the wind in Ezekiel 37:9-14 and John 3:8), the impulse of a sempiternal Desire in direct opposition to the entropic pull of stasis. It is dynamic and changeable.

Water too changes from liquid to vapor, to ice, to snow, and the distinct words we have for each of those states enable us to know exactly what is being described. Unfortunately, when we hear or read the word "spirit," the imagery we conjure, or concept we sketch, will very likely differ from that which the speaker or writer intended to convey.

Spirit is polymorphous, alternating between forms, and evolving from one state to a new one. At every step its manifestation and shape differ while remaining of a same nature. Spirit follows the circular run of reality and does not have a beginning or end, but we can trace its multiple hues from their origin in the "father" (see Logion 15).

Thomas reflects on the development of humanity through sempiternal Desire. Paired dynamically against the pull of stasis, a spark (fire is another frequent analogy for the spirit—see Logion 10) of godhood precipitates the emergence of the cosmos, carrying along a psychic thrust, sustainer of the life trapped into matter. Evolution occurs through the continued interplay of entropy and life's drive. Thus do living things develop and evolve, and the flesh comes into being "because of spirit." But the true wonder is the coming of spirit "into being because of the body." How can the flesh (body) give rise to the spirit from which it proceeds? How can spirit come into being if it already exists?

The spirit aspect that arises from the flesh is evolved. When the consciousness of sentient beings focuses into awareness and self-awareness, a marvel occurs. The psychic thrust transmutes into the *syzygos* to guide our self-reflecting individuality farther on the path of godhood. When the soul sees her reflection in the depths, spirit surfaces metamorphosed as a living eidolon that seeks emancipation from the lower plane and becomes the savior twin who will make our memories his own. The anamnesis then leaves the decaying body of flesh and bones to be received into an ethereal body. The soul has wedded her mystical consort, and from their love is born a holy child, the twy-formed god from whom they originated in the cycle of reality.

From the spirit to flesh to Spirit, the cycle closes itself. Reality is the constant flow of the divine, the sempiternal Desire, the "great wealth" placed into the "poverty" of matter and flesh, returning transmuted to its source. The "flesh coming into being because of spirit" is the descent of the spirit into the physical world, the projection of the "I AM" onto the material plane; the "spirit coming into being because of the body" is the *syzygos* who has begun his ascent out of matter.

Dyadicity and Triadicity - Logion 30

> *Jesus said: "(In) the place where there are three gods, they are in god (alt. "they are gods/the divinity"). (In) the*

> *place where there are two or one, I myself exists with him."*

With three claims, Thomas addresses dyadicity and triadicity as pertaining to divine destiny:

1. Where there are three gods, they are the divinity.
2. Where there are two (gods), the "living one" is with those two.
3. Where there is one (god), the "living one" is with that one.

We can infer the meaning of the three propositions above from what we have learned so far from Thomas:

- The three are the soul, the savior twin, and the twy-formed god arisen from their confluence (see Logion 16). Together, they form the divine triad.
- The two are the *syzygos* and the soul. The "living one" is "with them" as the eidolon within (see Logion 22).
- The one, then, is the soul herself who is divine by virtue of her rapture in the embrace of the savior twin. The soul's destiny is prefigured in the tale of Psyche unto whom Zeus bestowed divinity so she might remain with Eros on Olympus.

The awe-inspiring pronouncement of Logion 30 is that we are the twy-formed god, the "I am," the one and the many who stands at the beginning and the end. The same idea is found in Psalm 82: 6,

> *I have said, Ye are gods; and all of you are children of the most High.*

God is simultaneously us and always with us.

Sharing Gnosis - Logion 31

> *Jesus said: "No prophet is accepted in his (own) village; no physician heals those who know him."*

The next three logia expound on the responsibility of the *gnostici* to share with others that which they know about the salvation of the soul. However, this cannot be done haphazardly. Nothing spoils the sacred nature of a revelation more than zealous proselytizing. Thomas cautioned prudence (Logion 93), and his own gospel is shrouded in veiled words, secrecy, and mysteries. We should not assume our kin, friends and family will be interested in, let alone embrace our vision of truth. Nor should we think that the numinous realities we understand will necessarily heal those close to us who are spiritually ill. As it happens, the reverse is true. Thomas was aware of the psychological reality that people would sooner accept an answer or a remedy from a stranger with an aura of expertise than from someone they know too well.

The Radiance of Gnosis - Logion 32

> *Jesus said: "A fortified city built upon a peak cannot fall, nor can it be hidden."*

The salvific knowledge must be shared unceasingly to allow the souls of mankind to escape the material world. However, it is also inherently dangerous (and arrogant) to claim one's brand of truth as a universal verity and strive to impose one's belief system on any segment of a society. The *Tao Te Ching* is a wise counsel:

> *Those who know don't talk. Those who talk don't know. Close your mouth, block off your senses, blunt your sharpness, untie your knots, soften your glare, settle your dust. This is the primal identity. Be like the Tao. It can't be approached or withdrawn from, benefited or harmed, honored or brought into disgrace. It gives itself up continually. That is why it endures.* **(Emphases are mine.)**

This saying from the East is in tune with the intent of Logion 32: the light of truth shines on its own. Once the dualist mystic is imbued with the living eidolon within, he stands like a luminous city on a high mountain: those who never stop looking (see Logion 2) cannot miss its gates and watchtowers; and the "truthful and believing hearts" will seek the safety of its ramparts.

The Lamp of Gnosis - Logion 33

> *Jesus said: "That to which you will listen in your ear [and?] in the other ear (alt. "<u>in one of your ears</u>"), preach upon your housetops. No one lights a lamp and puts it under (a) [?] nor does he put it in a hidden place; instead, he puts it on the stand so that anyone who comes in and goes out may see its light (alt. may look at its light)."*

I suggest that the idiom "to preach over the rooftops"— that is to proclaim something to whomever can hear it— is a corruption of the original intent in the scriptures. Matthew wrote:

> *Whatever I tell you in the dark, speak in the light; and what you hear in the ear, preach on the housetops.*
>
> —Matthew 10: 27

This is congruent with the context of the gospel of Thomas. If Jesus taught his closest disciples in confidence, there is no rationale for them to preach the veiled teachings to the whole wide world (see also Logion 13).

At the time of Jesus in Palestine, rooftops were typically converted into terraces (as they still are nowadays in many Mediterranean and eastern countries) for family and small social gatherings, or even to sleep during the hottest night of the year (note the reference to the "dark" in Matthew 10:27 above, which could suggest intimate discussions taking place on one's rooftop and extending into the hours of the night). To "preach upon one's rooftop," then, would be to share only with a chosen few that which has been received in one's ear in contradiction to the gospel's commission:

> *Go ye therefore, and teach all nations ... to observe all things whatsoever I have commanded you.*
>
> —Matthew 28: 19-20

Matthew is not consistent on secrecy, but Thomas is.

It is the way of the *psychici* to rush and spread on everyone's else rooftops what they assume they know. This ill-conceived missionary approach has always had unforeseen disastrous consequences. The chosen prefer to stay home and keep by their side a lamp, the light of which "everyone who comes in and goes out" can see.

Beware of the Blind - Logion 34

> *Jesus said: "If a blind man leads a blind man, they both fall into a pit."*

Light in its literal and figurative aspects is a recurring motif in Thomas' gospel because the ethereality (behind and beyond) the physical world is luminous literally and metaphorically. Earlier we learned about acquiring the numinous insight (Logion 26) and "being a light unto the world" (Logia 24, 33). Logion 34 now warns us about the "blinds who lead the blinds," a metaphor for those lacking numinous discernment who nevertheless set themselves up as religious leaders and spiritual teachers.

On the road to Damascus, Saul was struck with blindness by the god he was called to serve. Remarkably, the founder of Christianity whose creed is followed by hundreds of millions of adherents began his apostolic career blinded by a flash "from the sky" (let us remember here that the mystical sovereignty is not in the sky—see Logion 3). He saw the brilliance that robbed him from the light, and one can only hope Paul's temporary blindness allowed him to find his inner vision before engaging in missionary work. The "person of light," however, has no need to lead or guide: "they light up the whole world" (see Logion 24). Moths are attracted to the dazzling light of the candle that burn them, but the seeker with "eyes to see" will recognize the ethereal "light shining in the darkness" within.

Staying Vigilant - Logion 35

> *Jesus said: "No one can go into a strong (person's) house and take it (alt. him) by force unless he binds his hands; then he will move out of his house."*

Logion 35 sees the return of the archons—the "thieves" we encountered in Logion 21—who attempt to break into the house (our body, the abode of the soul), and drive a wedge between the anamnesis held by the mind and the *syzygos* in order to exploit our memories they need for their collective sense of identity. The archons also seek to occupy our subconscious as a platform to multiply and gain strength. The looters' strategies are many and their task is easier when our "hands are tied," a metaphor for attachment to worldly matters.

Nowadays we live in a state of perpetual distraction: on top of our traditional concentric world of family, work, church, hobbies, entertainment, etc., we are ensnared in a new digital sphere, as witnessed by our addiction to portable electronic devices. The little time we once had to free the mind while resting, driving, walking, we now relinquish to the artificial intelligence. With our awareness effectively redirected away from our inner center, we neglect to notice the intruder lurking in a dark corner of our psyche. The masters of the material realm have bound our minds to do as they please in our home. Only sustained vigilance and persistence in holding the living eidolon in our heart can ensure the soul will bond with her savior twin and escape the clutches of the physicality. If the strong relaxes his guard, the archons intrude. This is particularly manifest when the mind loses its grip on the subconscious while the connection between Soul and *syzygos* is still tenuous as it is the case in dreams and other altered states of consciousness. When the *syzygos* attempts to take flight but the soul is still trapped, the archons invade the subconscious.

Detachment - Logion 36

> *Jesus said: "Do not take care from morning to evening and from evening to morning for that which you will put upon yourselves. <u>He it is who will give you your clothing</u> (†)."*

We just learned how commonplace distractions may cause us to relax our mindful vigilance and spiritual resolve, putting us in real danger to open the door of our innermost to the archons. Logion 36 continues in the same vein of thought. Easing our concerns about trivial, earthly matters is sound advice but, like other aphorisms in the gospel of Thomas, this saying reaches deeper than its most apparent intent. At a later date, the redactors of the New Testament would seize on these few words and build on them (see Luke 12:22) to fashion a broader context of divine providence. The idea was to discourage the destitute from seeking a higher status in society and encourage them to develop faith in the fatherly benevolence of a mythological god who provides for his children. The most diligent followers are always subservient and full of hope. The Gospel of Thomas gives no indication of such god because the chosen show no inclination to rely with blind faith on a condescending supreme cosmic being. They take care of themselves to the best of their ability; they understand the delicate balance between making one's sojourn on Earth bearable, or even pleasant, while remaining detached from the pursuit of material gains and avoiding the pitfall of mundane entanglements. They know that the excessive apprehension, worry, envy, and other negative emotional buildups from an obsessive quest for goods or influence form the subconscious ground from which the archons arise.

Worry from morning to evening elicits agitated dreams during the night, and disturbing dreams are the bailiwick of the archons. Of all the tricks to alter our dreams, none is wisest than finding serenity by day: the stillness of our conscious mind can tame nightly disquietude. Conversely, sleepless, anxiety-filled nights compromise our bodily system and mental health, making us more susceptible to unwanted, aggressive, and detrimental intrusions. Sleep deprivation is a proven method of torture. Lack of reparative rest is one of the greatest hazards (conveniently overlooked) of a modern world that keeps us on the edge with a purpose to induce in us a state of servility and receptivity to all sorts of suggestions.

We built an industrialized civilization only to be turned into the powerless consumers and slaves of the dystopian system we created. We keep generating unnecessary needs only to find ourselves worrying all day long about fulfilling them. When the mind is overly distracted and perturbed, the living eidolon is overshadowed; when the mind is silent, the *syzygos* strengthens and grows.

† This added reference to a god who provides for his children introduces an idea that is otherwise utterly absent from the gospel of Thomas. It marks a shift toward the god of the later Christians who believed the supreme deity was distinct, benevolent, and constantly involved in the lives of his creatures.

However, the "clothing" here could also represent the "robe of glory" (Logion 84), the etherealized body that envelops our soul in the transcendent eternity. The extended logion would in that case remains consistent with the teachings of Thomas: there is really no need to worry about the literal or figurative (see Logion 21) clothing we wear because both will vaporize with death. But "he it is"—the savior twin in the heart of the truthful (Logion 70)—who will give the saved souls their permanent, luminous raiment.

The Son of the Living One - Logion 37

> His disciples asked: "On what day will you appear to us, and on what day will we look upon you?" Jesus replied: "When you strip yourselves naked without being ashamed, taking your clothes and laying them under your feet like those little children, and you trample them, then [you will look upon]

> *the son of the living one, and you will not be afraid."*

With Logion 21 we examined the symbolism of children and the clothes they wear as representing the souls encased in bodies of flesh and bones. Logion 37, then, is an allegory for the souls rejecting the physical body to free themselves from the cast of matter. He who lives is either the savior twin, or the chosen in whose heart he has made his dwelling (see note 1 on Logion 0). The soul who favors the *syzygos* over her carnal envelope will soon enter an eternal and blessed henosis with her luciform companion. The figurative offspring resulting from that union is the "son of the living one," the holy child, or twy-formed god. Similarly, the man of light (see Logion 24) who is alive amidst the darkness of the world turns inwardly to give birth to his ethereal twin (see logion 4).

The disciples naively believe in the coming of a messiah on Earth, and their subsequent "rapture" to meet the Father in the heavens. The modern *psychici*—Mormons, Evangelists, Jehovah's Witnesses, Muslims, or Jews— entertain the same beliefs in an incarnate redeemer they expect to return in apocalyptic fashion and are looking forward to a day of reckoning and apotheosis. But the revelation of the "son of the living one" is not a day of retribution and fear. The millenarists do not understand the soul is the liberator of the savior twin who stands to release her from the burden of matter. In mutual embrace, they cannot fear. Only the false god of the Abrahamists demands to be feared and threatens his "children" with wrath if they do not comply.

The Source of Gnosis - Logion 38

> *Jesus said: "Many times you were desirous to listen to these words I spoke to you, and you did not have another one from whom to hear them. The days are coming you will seek after me (but) will not find me."*

The Jesus in the gospel of Thomas is not the Messiah but a literary, allegorical figure for the true source of the salvific knowledge that lies in our innermost (see Appendix 1) There is no incarnate substitute for the guide within. Thomas reveals gnostic principles to satisfy our yearning, but he points in the direction of the fountainhead before he too withdraws into the figurative. The search for a historical Thomas, or for a savior who once walked the dusty roads of Palestine is a futile endeavor. Our salvation rests not in anyone visible among our kind, but in "giving birth to the one in ourselves" (see Logion 70).

Finding the Knowledge Within - Logion 39

> *Jesus said: "The Pharisees and the scribes took the keys of gnosis (and) hid*

them. They did not go in, and those who desire to go in they did not allow. You, however, be wise like serpents and innocent like doves."

In the wake of a warning in Logion 38 not to look for an "external" savior, Thomas claims that the Pharisees and the scribes (in our days they would be those who manage and manipulate religious beliefs) are not to be trusted as suitable guides. The keys of gnosis are its transformative powers. They are hidden when the esoteric and allegorical meaning of holy texts is ignored in favor of literal interpretations, barring those who regulate the flow of beliefs and their followers to undergo a salvific transformation (see Logion 67). Instead, they rely on theological systems that gives authority and prestige to a priesthood while the masses are fed simplistic crumbs of knowledge and think they are being empowered. The elite pontificates, lies to itself (see Logion 6), and misdirects the faithful away from the well (or spring) of the living water from which no one will drink (see Logia 28 and 74) because of folly or duplicity.

The transformative powers of gnosis are recovered when we bypass the intermediaries becoming "wise like serpents and innocent like doves." The pairing of those two animals symbolizes the Soul-*syzygos* dyad often represented by sacred twins in mythologies worldwide. Ancient Egyptians, for instance, worshipped the deities Tefnut and Shu who were born from the vital essence of the One God Atum.

"The lunar eye of Ra"—Tefnut—who takes the form of a cobra, is the soul. As the snake is closest to earth (the sublunar plane), so is the soul—the child of memories—endowed with the wisdom of existential experience. The saying is also an implicit recognition of the serpent not as the deceitful villain of the Abrahamists, but as the wise figure who offered Eve (she represents the soul) the gnosis to liberate herself from the tyranny of the false god (the demiurge who walked in the garden of Eden).

"He who rises up"—Shu—the air god whose emblems are the feathers, is the savior twin, the spirit who comes into being because of the body (see Logion 29), the child of life. "The wind bloweth where it listeth, and thou hearest the sound thereof, but canst not tell whence it cometh, and whither it goeth: so is every one that is born of the Spirit," says the apostle John. Thus, the traditional symbol for the spirit is a dove, the air creature who embodies childlike freedom and insouciance.

Such are the transformative keys found in the stillness of one's heart: the freedom of the dove, and the wisdom of the serpent.

The Spiritually Malnourished - Logion 40

Jesus said: "A vine of grapes planted outside of the father did not grow

> *strong. It will be pulled up by its root and destroyed."*

Logion 15 showed that the archetypal "Father" of the Judeo-Christian tradition is but the allegorical embodiment of a psychic thrust that sustains the world and nourishes the souls during their sojourn on Earth, and until they are released from the world of matter. Who then is "planted outside the father?" The *psychici* and the *hylici* respectively put their faith in distorted, misleading spiritual teachings, or in worldly constructs. Their individualities do not persist beyond death: the psychic thrust returns to its source, and, as the memories quickly disperse in matter, the souls fade out.

The Plenitude - Logion 41

> *Jesus said: "To him who has (something) in his hand will be given (more), and from him who does not have (something) will be taken even the little he has in his hand."*

The warning of the previous saying carries into Logion 41: The *psychici* and the *hylici* are the "malnourished" because they do not know where to find the keys of knowledge (see Logion 39). Without those keys, they cannot escape the realm of matter, and the little knowledge they acquired in their lifetime will amount to nothing. Only the *pneumatici* who constantly search the innermost depths of their being for nourishment will have "something in hand," to show at the crossing of the threshold between the sublunary and the etherealized (see Logion 50). They hold the keys of gnosis and will be given a hundredfold.

Life Is a Bridge- Logion 42

Jesus said: "Become passersby (alt. 'come into being as you pass away')."

Thomas' meditations are few but paramount. Rather than dwelling on lengthy doctrinal and metaphysical expositions, his gospel reveals the core of gnosis, the indispensable keys needed by the soul to find the *syzygos* and become a monad. The nature of those few keys is unveiled through illustrations that work on our mind from various angles until we can grasp the gist of the salvific knowledge.

The shortest saying in the Gospel of Thomas is also one of the weightiest. The passerby is insouciant and travels "light," unencumbered by possessions, free from the entanglements of the world (see Logion 36). His existence is a short, transitional crossing between no-being and god-being. Nothing can be taken away from this life except the remembrance of it. There is no resurrection of the body: it will be left behind to rot along with everything we accumulated, collected, saved, or built in the temporal realm (see also Logion 63). For all the esoteric keenness often attributed to the ancient Egyptians, they certainly were gravely mistaken thinking they could transfer into the beyond the lifestyle they enjoyed on the physical plane, complete with furniture, slaves, pets, and concubines.

On the main gateway of the Buland Darwaza in India, one can read, etched in the stone, an inscription commissioned by a ruler who, despite his exalted rank, understood the wisdom of the passerby:

> *Isa, son of Mary said: "The world is a Bridge, pass over it, but build no houses upon it. He who hopes for a day, may hope for eternity; but the World endures but an hour. Spend it in prayer for the rest is unseen.*

Across time and lands, the noēsis of Thomas is echoed by the Muslim king's motto enjoining the reader to relinquish the material sphere, prepare himself for what lies at the conclusion of the journey on the other end of the bridge, and become one's Self (come into being) through the act of passing by.

The Voice of Authority - Logion 43

> *His disciples said to him, "Who are you that you would say these things to us?" "From that which I tell you, you do not realize who I am. Rather, you have become like those Judeans. For (either) they love the tree and hate its fruit (or) they love the fruit (but) hate the tree."*

A striking aspect of man's search for meaning is his deep-seated need to find someone he can invest with the authority to tell him what he wants to know (or more likely what he wants to hear). One may claim to follow his own path and yet, will perpetually punctuate metaphysical ramblings with quotes of spiritual pundits, and let his steps be guided by the self-appointed experts of the unseen who have no valid claim of their expertise.

Previously, the disciples called their Master "a just angel" and "a wise philosopher" (see Logion 13) or mistook him for a messiah (see Logion 37); now they question his legitimacy. This vacillating reflects the religious climate in the time of Thomas but is also common in our days: innumerable factions vie for influence, arguing endlessly other contradictory lines of thought, swapping followers who keep changing their mind about whom or what to "like and follow."

From the esoteric standpoint, those who either love the tree and hate its fruit or love the fruit and hate the tree lack insight into the dyadic nature of man who is both father (the tree) and child (the fruit), the savior and the saved. Furthermore, there is no rationale for having to choose between either theism or a humanism because we are both the creator (the tree) and his creature (the fruit), a god-being everlastingly giving birth to himself. These conclusions align with Logion 3: those who seek the mystical sovereignty solely in outward theurgy, or by retreating exclusively into the psyche, may never find it until they realize what they sought is both within them and before their eye (see Logion 3).

Embracing Godhood - Logion 44

> *Jesus said: "He who blasphemes the father will be forgiven, and he who blasphemes the son will be forgiven. However, he who blasphemes the spirit who is holy will not be forgiven— neither on earth no) in heaven."*

There is in the traditional gospels a parallel to Logion 44 that generates much confusion among exegetes: how could blasphemy against the Holy Spirit be a greater sin than blaspheming the Father or the Son?

In the previous Logion we discovered there is no distinction between the "tree" (father) and the "fruit" (son), which are two aspects of the same reality. In Logia 15 and 16 we explored the allegorical use of father and son to represent the psychic thrust and the soul respectively, the dyad at the core of our being; and to blaspheme against our own nature is of no consequence. Christianity presents the Father as the supreme God who rules over the Son who confers the Holy Spirit. The members of the Christian Trinity figure in a hierarchy of authority and power, but the esoteric truth lies in a simile: the source that flows as two rivers that become one into the sea (†) after having washed over the land of the sensible world. As the son has his origin in the invisible father, the soul and her *syzygos* came into being because of the psychic thrust. And when the soul weds the savior twin, a holy child—the "spirit who is holy"—rises from their union (see Logion 37). To blaspheme against this holy child is to renounce one's godhood and the apotheosis of the Self, for which there is no pardon because it means the separation (see Logion 61) of the *syzygos* (returning to its source in "heaven," the luminous plenitude) and the soul (left wandering the physical plane as an individual's fragmented anamnesis) until a god-being dreams the same earthly vehicle in the new circumstances that allow for the re-unification of *syzygos* and Soul.

Alternatively, the "spirit" in Logion 44 can be understood as the pneuma itself, the divine breath that actualizes in stages culminating with the birth of the savior twin of the soul (Logion 10). The idea of the spirit as savior of the soul was central to the faith of the 12th century Cathars (see Logion 45 below) who preserved and adapted dualist, gnostic, and early Christian traditions. The Cathars regarded the true Father (††) as completely removed from the material plane and without any active role in the salvation of his children. No blasphemy on earth could possibly affect him. Jesus was his envoy to teach the salvific knowledge and give the sacrament of the *consolamentum* to mankind, but that was the extent of his mission: he had no further role in the redemption. When the Cathars were "consoled"—that is when they were given the *consolamentum*—they received the holy spirit (*spiritus sanctus*) as a companion until their higher Self (*spiritus angelicus*) could receive them in the afterlife. To blaspheme against this spirit then is to deny oneself a return to the **empyrean of the blessed**.

The notion that we have both a spirit and a soul was once widely accepted in Christianity until it was expurged from Christian beliefs by the Second Council of Constantinople in 553 C.E. Thomas, like the Manicheans and the Cathars after him, believed that spirit to be the savior of the soul. Linda Harris comments:

> *This Saviour may appear to be a separate entity, but he is actually the soul's own spirit. He descends from the world of light into the darkness of matter, in order to help the fallen soul. ... The idea that human beings had divine spirits, and could become divine themselves if their souls were reunited with these spirits, was presumably considered unacceptable because it diminished the unique status of Christ. It would also have conflicted with the Church's doctrine of salvation through grace.*
>
> —Linda Harris, *the Secret Heresy of Hieronymus Bosch*, second edition, 2002

—

† The sea eventually evaporates, falling back into the source as rain, thus perpetuating the self-sustaining cycle (see Logion 18).

†† The Cathars considered the "Father" of the Catholics to be Satan himself (*Satanel*, *Satanas*), the false god or demiurge.

The "Good People" - Logion 45

> *Jesus said: "Grapes are not harvested from thorns, and figs are not harvested from thistles; they do not produce fruit. A good man brings a good thing out of his treasure; an evil man brings evil things out of the wicked treasure in his heart (alt. 'in his mind'), and he speaks evil (because) from the excess of the mind he brings out evil things."*

The 12th century dualist Cathars called themselves "bons hommes" and "bonnes femmes"—the good people. They renounced the material world, its artifices, its ways of life, and its schemes. They were vegetarians (†), non-violent, earnest, and living simply. Their treasury was not a place in the world, but the vaulted chamber of the heart. Their influence on medieval society was stabilizing and helped foster a renaissance in 12th century southern France.

The Church of Rome with its appendant greed for power, authority, and possessions had assembled a treasure of evil. The infamous inquisition was originally created to destroy the Cathar "heresy" and hunt down its followers to the last. Slander, torture, threats, abuse, robbery, murder, nothing was too monstrous for a papacy with no interest in authentic values. Within a hundred years, the church of the pontiff and his cardinals eradicated the church of the *perfecti*, decimated the *credenti*, burned their sacred books, and erased their unique knowledge.

The tragedy of the Cathars is a striking illustration of Logion 45: a good people who *brought good things out of their treasure* pitted against those whose heart overflowed with evil, although they claimed to do good. There is no redemption for those who cannot make the difference.

—

† Although there may be many good reasons to be a vegetarian in the 21st century, by and large, vegetarians themselves overlook the mystical roots of vegetarianism when the practice was meant to distance the soul from the violence of the kill and to wash the taint of death off the divine essence. According to Porphyry in his exhaustive treatise *On Abstinence from animal food*, the newly initiated in the bacchanal rites would declare:

> *Clothed in pure white garments, I flee from the birth of mortals; I do not approach graves, and <u>I do not tolerate in my food anything which has lived</u>.*
> (Emphasis is mine.)
>
> —Quoted in Eugène Goblet d'Alviella, *Mysteries of Eleusis*.

Thus, vegetarianism is an additional step for the *pneumatici* who seek to rise above the material plane defined by cycles of birth, decay, and death. (See also Logia 7 and 11)

The Sovereign Child - Logion 46

> *Jesus said: "Among those born of women, from Adam to John the Baptist, no man is placed above John the Baptist, so that (one would) avert his eyes (from him). Yet I said: he among you who comes into being as a little one will know the mystical sovereignty and be placed above Johann."*

As great a prophet as John the Baptist might have been, the one who becomes a child is superior to him. We previously remarked (Logia 21, 22,37) how the state of childhood is an allegory denoting the characteristics of the soul and the *syzygos* respectively. Status, saintliness, faith, good works, all come to naught unless the soul ceases to identify with the mind and assimilates instead the archetype of the *puer aeternus*—the eternal child—empowering the living eidolon to mature into the savior twin of the soul. Together, the soul and her savior can escape the grasp of matter and give rise to the holy child who inherits the never-ending mystical sovereignty. Thus can the psalmist claims:

> *You are gods; you are all children of the Most High.*
> —Psalm 82:6

The Two Principles - Logion 47

> *Jesus said: "There is no way a man can mount two horses and stretch two bows, and there is no way a servant can serve two lords, or he will honor the one and the other he will despise. No man drinks aged wine and immediately desires to drink new wine. And they do not pour new wine into old wineskins lest they split; and they do not pour aged wine into new wineskins lest it go bad. And old patches are not sewn onto new garments because that would make a tear."*

Logion 47 uses short parables to expound the dynamics between the two opposite principles that characterize the tide of Apeiron and govern reality: the divine psychic thrust, and the pull of stasis, or entropy. A thousand years later, John of Lugio would preoccupy himself with the same propositions in his extensive treatise, *the Book of Two Principles*:

I wish to begin my discussion concerning the two principles by refuting the belief in one Principle, however much this may contradict well-nigh all religious persons. We may commence as follows: Either there is only one First Principle, or there is more than one. If, indeed, there were one and not more, as the unenlightened say, then, of necessity, He would be either good or evil. But surely not evil, since then only evil would proceed from Him and not good ... [This could not be] unless He were divided against Himself ... doing that which would be wholly contrary to Himself.

—Source: www.gnosis.org

The Cathar scholar spoke in terms understandable within the theological paradigm of his time, but we need to realize that good and evil are concepts with no existence outside the mind. They cannot cause anything because they are themselves the subjectively observable results of pre-existent antithetical processes. In an apologetic essay on dualism, Ernst Jonson wrote:

The actual world evidently arises from the interaction of two opposite principles. One of these principles is mechanical and destructive. The other principle is creative; and therefore it cannot be regarded as mechanical, but it must be regarded as intelligent.

—The Monist, Vol. 28, No. 4, October, p. 626

We live in a fantasy world seen through carefully crafted lenses. Conceptual fabrications make us feel endowed with the responsibility to defend a benevolent natural order against an imaginary nefarious entity. Our fight becomes moral and we seek to promote what we perceive as good and thwart what we believed is evil. We are blindsided by a purpose-driven life where we are the free agents of the ultimate triumph of goodness. But the struggle never was between good and evil, and we do not actually fight in the battle that unfolds on its own in the center of our own being.

Humans are the battlefield for a titanic difluence, the bifurcating ground where matter and physical life have their origins. The world and its inhabitants were born of the very opposition that tears them apart. For as long as we *mount two horses, stretch two bows, and serve two lords*, we are subjected to mortality. "A house divided against itself cannot stand" (see Mark 3:25), and we are doomed to destruction unless we escape the material universe by surrendering to the tides of Apeiron and giving birth to the Self Triumphant.

* * *

Interestingly, centuries before the gospel of Thomas was written, the Dhammapada beautifully and concisely expressed an idea we can read as the synthesis of logia 45 and 47:

> *With themselves as their own enemies, fools lacking in intelligence, move about doing evil deeds, which bear bitter fruits.* (v. 66)

Moving Mountains - Logion 48

> *Jesus said: "If two make peace with one another in this one house, they will tell the mountain, 'move away!' and it will move."*

This Logion can only be understood metaphorically: no matter how peaceful a household is, it will never literally displace mountains. Thus, the saying confirms that the image of the house in the gospel of Thomas (see Logia 16, 21, and 35) does not refer to a man-made edifice of stone and wood. And when Jesus speaks of "this one house, we can imagine him pointing at his own body of flesh that houses the mind, the soul and the living eidolon. This home of ours is profoundly divided: on the one hand, our mind and our body are torn by the two great opposing forces of life and entropy (see Logion 47); on the other hand, the *syzygos* and the soul are kept separated in the labyrinthine dwellings of our inner being. When the separation vanishes, the lover and the Beloved flee to a place of light to give birth to the twy-formed god. It is he who has the power to shape his mystical sovereignty at will, moving the mountains of the new, luminous, etherealized kingdom he creates (manifests) for himself.

Determinism and the Cycle of Reality - Logion 49

> *Jesus said: "Blessed are the monad and the chosen, because you will find the mystical sovereignty. For you are from it, (and) you will return again to it."*

Logion 49 introduces the principle of determinism while reiterating the circular nature of reality. An understanding of those two notions leads to a realization of how the divine destiny of mankind unfolds.

Those who are "monad" and "chosen" (see also Logion 23) are the *pneumatici*: they surrender their soul to the savior twin and rise with him as the twy-formed god. They are chosen not by virtue of any god's arbitrary decree but because, through the eons, the creative intent of the sempiternal Desire shaped their individualities as the right vehicle for an assured victory over entropy. The living eidolon finds in the elect a truthful heart where to dwell and an altar at which the soul and her savior twin are joined to enter the mystical sovereignty (see Logion 3).

To be among the chosen is not a matter of self-righteousness or eclecticism. The chosen recognize themselves simply because of a fervent desire above all else to be released from the bounds of matter and physicality. Honestly, how often will you hear someone claiming his craving to be free from the clutches of physicality (unless one intends to scare away friends, family, or co-workers)? The chosen are silent, but they have one dominant drive: the release of their soul in the embrace of one's *syzygos*. That is what makes them the *pneumatici*.

Whether or not we are among the "chosen," we all originate from the same place: we emerged from the mystical sovereignty of the god-being. Eventually each parcel of pneuma that has entered the realm of matter through many rounds will ebb into its own source accompanied by a divinely anointed soul. This is the circular nature of reality we discussed in Logia 18 and 29.

The annular wandering of pneuma has a paramount implication: determinism. Not only *are we from it and will again return to it*, but we stand simultaneously at the beginning and the end of the journey (see Logion 18). We are gods, we are eternal, and we perpetuate our divinity through cycles of re-manifestation. From the beginning we know how it ends, but that omniscience is lost in the pattern of renewal and rebirth. We are a story that has already been written; only from our mortal perspective it seems to unfold unpredictably. At any point of eternity, we are looking through a different window. Some windows afford a better view than others, but the landscape has always been the same and we are seeing it from multiple angles with us in it at different stages of our numinous evolution.

The Return to the Light - Logion 50

> *Jesus said: "If they ask you, 'Whence have you come?' tell them, 'We came from the light, the place where the light came into being on its own.' He stood upright and appeared in their image. If they ask you, 'Are you he?' say, 'We are his sons, and we are the chosen of the father who lives.' If they ask you, 'What is the sign of your father within you?' tell them, 'It is a movement and a repose.'"*

With Logion 50 we reach the theurgical core of the gospel of Thomas. It recapitulates crucial principles we explored earlier, condensing them into three short allegorical dialogs between the "chosen" (see Logion 49) who are journeying back to the heavenly light and some mysterious interlocutors. In gnostic mythology, the interrogators are the archons who act as guardians of the physical universe—hiding in its supersensible dimensions—and are the jailers of our divine essence.

Likely, this spoken exchange was once performed in the initiation phase of a religious mystery: the epopt would recite formulas in answer to key questions before being admitted to the other side of a veil. The ceremony prefigured the passage of the chosen from the physical world to the veiled, invisible "place of light." On the way, they would have to face figuratively the custodians of the cosmos and foil their last attempt at preventing the release of the soul from the shackles of materiality. The archons are powerless against the *pneumatici* who have received gnosis, the salvific knowledge reflected in the replies they give to the occult rulers soon to be defeated.

The reply to the archons' first query was examined in Logion 49: we (all) came from the "place of light," a luminous, transcendent milieu that renews itself through pneuma, and the descent of divine sparks into physicality where human bodies are created in the image of the god-being. In the sensible realm, pneuma manifests itself first as the psychic thrust that sustains our carnal bodies, and subsequently absorbs the human soul to ascend as Desire triumphant and return to its birthplace as the renewed twy-formed god.

The reflection of the soul into the innermost is the living eidolon, the manifestation of the invisible father in the heart of the truthful (see also Logion 59). "Are you he?" ask the archons. The initiate answers that he is the child of the "living one" (see Logion 15).

The archons then ask a third and last question to test the understanding of the chosen, hoping to weaken their resolve and steer them away from the royal gate. But the destiny of the *pneumatici* is sealed: they slip past the theocratic keepers and escape the realm of the dead. Through their intimacy with the *syzygos*, they comprehend the entirety as the eternal cycle of movement followed by repose (see Logion 18). Having overcome the pull of stasis, they are ready to enter the empyrean of the blessed—a scene astoundingly represented in the *Ascent of the Blessed* painted by Hieronymus Bosch.

The Everlasting Mystical Sovereignty - Logion 51

> *His disciples asked him: "On what day will the repose of the dead be, and on what day will the new world come?" He replied: "That which you are looking for (out there) has come. Nevertheless, you do not see it."*

Whereas the *pneumatici* find the inner byways to repose in the empyrean of the blessed, the *psychici* tread the earthy, dusty roads of dogma and belief systems, or follow the endless paths of self-proclaimed swamis, gurus, spiritual teachers, prophets, occult masters, magi, and "channelers."

No sooner has Jesus opened the gates to wonders hitherto unthinkable for the human soul than the disciples revert to their usual errors. They still cannot fathom the possibility of the mystical sovereignty within and prefer to inquire about a hypothetical, theocratic new world, and the resurrection of the dead when the departed are back to mingle with the living—the same tales the neo-

Christians of the 21st century continue to peddle to their children. One can almost sense exasperation in the answer of a patient tutor: there is no paradisiacal order coming to Earth in spectacular ways; it is not "out there" but within, and they cannot see it.

The Living One - Logion 52

> *His disciples said to him: "Twenty-four prophets in Israel have spoken, and all of them spoke of in you." He said to them: "You have ignored the living one in your presence, and you have spoken of those who are dead."*

In this Logion and the next, the disciples continue to preoccupy themselves with the rites, customs, and traditions of human religion rather than seeking the revelation of their own heart. Followers are always in need of reaffirmation from religious authorities and, in this instance, they want a confirmation their teacher is the promised Messiah (see also Logion 43). But those who made such promise were dead spiritually before they died physically. Their prophecies are obsolete because they were deaf to the call of the *syzygos*. The *psychici* rely on the dead and ignore the living eidolon right in front of them (as in a mirror)—not Jesus, Thomas, or any other than the guide within, the savior twin rising from the depths.

Circumcision in Spirit - Logion 53

> *His disciples said to him: "Is circumcision beneficial to us, or not?" He said to them: "If it were beneficial, their father would beget them (already) circumcised from their mother. Nevertheless, the true circumcision in spirit has become entirely beneficial."*

Wherever we seek the origin of, or a justification for the custom of circumcision, the barbaric practice means only one thing: subservience. In the pre-industrial world, slaves and defeated enemies were branded by the removal of their prepuce. The Egyptian elite used the same to show their own fanatical submissiveness to the gods who would grant them in the life beyond the same privileges they enjoyed in their earthly existence. The Hebrews got the idea from Egypt and made it the mark of allegiance to their own demiurge. And under the guise of misguided claims of health and hygiene (a case of weird science), circumcision still has proponents within the 21st century medical establishment of many countries with a cultural bias for conformity. In all instances, the circumcised male makes a sacrifice of flesh and blood to his worldly rulers and cosmic masters.

Self-maiming as a sign of subservience epitomizes a slave culture that stands in contrast to the liberation of the individual promulgated by Thomas. True freedom comes from surrendering one's mind and soul—a "circumcision in spirit"—to the "living one." Circumcision of the flesh is an abomination despised in Thomas' time by the more enlightened Hellenists whose mental, abstract acuity could not fathom a ritualistic mutilation for the sake of pleasing a vulgar god.

Voluntary Frugality - Logion 54

> *Jesus said: "Blessed are the poor, for the mystical sovereignty of heaven is yours."*

Poverty is not a blessed condition but can be a blessing. There is no reason the poor should not apply themselves to seeking the means of escaping indigence, but they must do so without jeopardizing what should be the cardinal enterprise of life, the realization of the mystical sovereignty within. In that aspect, being poor has an advantage over being rich: goods, properties, and money inevitably build up into walls of materialism that encircle the soul in a donjon. The legitimate efforts to improve one's lot can just as easily turn into greed and materialistic fixations.

The rich enjoy circumstances of comfort and ease that afford them the leisure of loftier endeavors, but they rarely have an interest in metaphysical concerns. The poor who must strain and struggle to make ends meet and survive have little resources left they can dedicate to spiritual pursuits. Thus, a class-oriented society is inherently not conducive to mystical aspirations. Instead, such a society fosters adherence to collective creeds and *prêt-à-porter* religions that do not require independent thinking but allay spiritual thirst to some extent. The leading denominations ensure the status quo is preserved because they receive the monetary support of the wealthy and the protection of the powerful. The lower classes at the base of the system are offered dubious hope and reassurance that obedience, faith, and hard work will ultimately be rewarded in this life or the next.

We are not blessed when forced into misery by an absurd, unfair, and elitist economic rationale, but when we voluntarily choose frugality and put limits on our possessions and revenues. This does not involve extreme asceticism or deprivation, but a great presence of mind to stop following institutionalized rapacity, chasing after ever greater profits, and hoarding goods. A decreased involvement in materialistic aims fosters the attention we give to the welfare of our soul. Such is the blessing of the poor who inherit the mystical sovereignty; otherwise Logion 54 would be just an empty promise to keep the disadvantaged into subservience.

Poverty may not be a guaranty of piety but, unsurprisingly, tribal societies without a class structure based on ownership and the accumulation of property show a keener connection to the supersensible realm and a greater satisfaction in life than does the modern man in his daily "pursuit of happiness." The unseen realm pervades and shapes the life of the tribe in such ways they have no need for industrialization, economic theories, and capital. They implement communal stewardship, plucking off the land only that which they need and sharing fairly. Without class distinction, they see no rationale for upward mobility. Without attributing meaning to material wealth, they find significance in their relationships to a transcendent realm.

Family Ties - Logion 55

> *Jesus said: "Whoever does not hate his father and his mother cannot become a disciple to me, (and) he (who) does not hate his brothers and his sisters (and) does not take up his cross like me, to me, he will not become deserving."*

Logion 55 presents a challenge to the 21st century communities that emphasize the two-parent family as the building block of society and attach "moral values" to this very modern cultural organization (the tribe, or clan is in fact the natural and most common arrangement for the community life of mankind). This saying might have been controversial even for the early Christians. The Evangelist Luke reproduces it almost verbatim (Luke 14:26) but his counterpart Matthew takes care to alter the wording and lessen the impact of the admonition (see Matthew 10:37). The stark advice leaves the neo-Christians in a quandary and at pains to explain what their savior could have intended to say. They often circumvent the dilemma in the same way we excuse a politician's outlandish claims: "He was exaggerating to make a point." But Thomas and Luke meant what they wrote: family ties are an impediment to transcendental progress. The two apostles do not hate any one member of the family but loathe the social construct which is an artificial arrangement forced upon free individuals to bend them to subservience. It is indeed in the heart of the household system that the rules and rationales of the social order are initially inculcated and promulgated by the rulers. Our masters do not want us to understand Luke literally, for they know a rejection of the smallest social component would tear apart the cohesive structure of control they have established over us. Meanwhile, neo-Christian detractors of Thomas are quick to point out the anti-marriage, anti-family nature of his gospel as if it were an affront to human dignity. The truth however is that there is nothing morally superior in being pro-marriage or pro-family. Jiddu Krishnamurti is one rare, authentic mystic who did not shy away from revealing the true nature of our beloved institutions:

Your parents are frightened, your educators are frightened, the governments and religions are frightened of your becoming a total individual, because they all want you to remain safely within the prison of environmental and cultural influences. But it is only the individuals who break through the social pattern by understanding it, and who are therefore not bound by the conditioning of their own minds - it is only such people who can bring about a new civilization, not the people who merely conform, or who resist one particular pattern because they are shaped by another. The search for God or truth does not lie within the prison, but rather in understanding the prison and breaking through its walls.

The family is an agent of conformity and an obstacle to the realization of the transcendentally sovereign individual.

* * *

The so-called fundamental unit of society as understood in the industrialized world is but an incubator for neuroses. In tribal societies, infants typically have several "mothers" sharing the burden of raising anyone's progeny. Children form bands without parental supervision, unhampered to roam and play on their own, learning together the patterns and cycles of their environment. Subsequently, the Elders and the wisest of the tribe show the adolescents the ways of life and the mysteries of the earthly and supersensible realms. Thus, the members of the tribe are spared most of the mental aberrations displayed in "civilized" nations.

The World of the Dead - Logion 56

Jesus said: "Whoever has known the world has found a corpse, and whoever has found a corpse, the world is not worthy of him."

Our universe and our planet are dead even as they harbor life. Earth is a tomb for the true life of which organic life is a mere by-product. The psychic thrust pervades the earthy shell, but only when it breaks out of its carapace will it develop as infinite life. The soul herself is prisoner of the body, and her destiny is to leave the corpse behind and join her savior twin in a henosis that will free both from the grasp of physicality (see Logion 4). The *gnostici* realize there is nothing of true value in earthly life, save the soul. What we call our home is a field that does not belong to us (see Logion 21), and our carnal envelope is a garment fit to be trampled under one's feet (see Logion 37). Once *syzygos* and soul are sealed to one another, they abandon the world of matter that inevitably decays like a rotting cadaver. "Let the dead bury their own dead," claims the Evangelist (see Luke 9:60), signifying that those who bury their dear ones are metaphorically no more alive than the departed.

What do people mean when they say unreflectively "it's good to be alive?" Did they just have a brush with death that triggered their inborn instinct to stay alive at any cost? Did they enjoy a turn of luck from which they derive material benefits? Did they find themselves in such happy circumstances they can forget the horror they witnessed before and the despair that could still invade them at any time? Was their brain flooded with the feel-good neurochemicals our body is able to produce? Or, was the unfathomable circuitry of the mind suddenly selecting their most satisfying memories while eliding the unpleasant ones? If it is good to be alive at this instant, will the feeling persist tomorrow when hardship, affliction, or disaster strikes randomly?

Have you ever heard a child claiming that it is good to be alive? (Unless, obviously, he is parroting.) Children cannot think of something so ridiculous: when they are jubilant, they delight in the experience without making pronouncements of dubious validity; when they hurt, they suffer without asking why misfortune befell them. Furthermore, if life is a school, as so many believe, why are the tutorials mostly painful? Don't we learn far better and faster by positive reinforcement than through punishing means? Only adults who do not pause an instant to think about what they are saying (or otherwise who have a vested interest in making us believe that which is contrary to what we can observe) would describe the sublunary world in glowing terms. And they do it without a care for the evidence that our days are more distressful than blissful (as Gautama Buddha discovered as soon as he escaped his golden cage). Where is the goodness in aliveness? Life is not a gift (from whom exactly?), it is a necessity. It has no purpose, no meaning, but is has an unbending intent.

When we are fortunate enough, for a passing moment, to glimpse a parcel of preternatural beauty trapped in the world; when we are overwhelmed by incomprehensible joy, empathy, or compassion, we are in harmony with the god-essence that streams through the cosmos in a rush to escape its confines. It has never been good to be alive physically, it is good to be alive spiritually. Whosoever wants a part in the empyrean above must forgo his stake in the world below.

The Seed of Gnosis - Logion 57

> *Jesus said: "The mystical sovereignty of the father is like a man who had [good] seed. His enemy came by night and sowed weeds among the good seed. The man did not let them pull out the weeds. He said to them: 'Lest you go to pull out the weeds (and end up) pulling up the grain with it. On the day of the harvest (when) the weeds are*

> *discernible, they pull them up and burn them.'"*

I read a thousand books in my life, the bulk of them being of religious, spiritual, esoteric, occult, and mystical nature. I went to church too. I listened to peoples' ideas on different continents, in several nations and islands. I learned and I reflected; I believed and I doubted; I accepted and I rejected.

I trust most of the teachers who influenced my thinking were sincere; I am now convinced they were also mostly misguided. A handful of good seeds grew with a profusion of weeds, but I could not make the difference. Only with patience and perseverance can we sift out the nourishing knowledge from the useless or poisonous one. There is no shortcut to the harvest, and those who speak the contrary are misleading their audience with books to study, precepts to follow, behaviors to adopt, beliefs to assimilate, and techniques to master. These preachers in all places are the adversaries of our soul. Time is our friend. The gathering of the fruits comes when they are ripe, and the most powerful realizations arrive in the latter years. Consistency is our ally. The harvest will be sterile though unless we tend the garden: pruning, watering, fertilizing, keeping bugs and disease at bay, etc. "He who seeks, let him not stop seeking until he finds" (Logion 2). When we "find," we will notice the weeds to toss them in the fire. The mystical sovereignty is not a place (see Logion 3) but a state of radiant gnosis, a window opening from inside the conditional world and into a dimension of infinite marvel.

On one level then, Logion 57 is about knowledge; but it also makes use of the imagery that recalls the parable in Logion 9, which taught how some seeds of pneuma end up being choked by thorns. The enemies of the soul (see Logion 21) are using a strategy of spreading lies and half-truths to steer her away from the path of release. Meanwhile, the suffocating proximity of the weeds threatens to stunt the growth of the savior twin and prevent his ascendency over the soul. There is however a safer and more fruitful alternative to picking the truth out of the swamp of falsehood: when we nourish the living eidolon with great care, we soon learn to recognize its shapes, modes of influence, and effects on our mind, and we become the recipient of transcendental wisdom.

Worth the Trouble - Logion 58

> *Jesus said: "Blessed is the man who has been troubled; he has found life."*

As we stressed in our exploration of the previous Logion, the "harvest" will be poor unless some work is done. Yet, there are those who promise we can relax our way to Nirvana or be saved by welcoming Jesus as our savior. "He who seeks, let him not stop seeking until he finds," tells Logion 2. That is our toil commensurable with the reward of "reigning over the entirety." Wondrous insights and powerful realizations come to the *gnostici* who have dedicated their life to unveiling the mysteries of the mystical sovereignty and searching the depths of their being instead of taking for granted the promises of books, priests and pastors, or uncritically accepting the voice of self-proclaimed Masters and Teachers.

Another reading of this saying is related to Logion 56. Life on Earth is characterized by labor and suffering more than ease and joy but, advancing steadily through the difficulties can illumine the veritable nature of our existence. With a new understanding of our earthly circumstances, we may find the truer life of the everlasting god-being.

The Pursuit of the Living One - Logion 59

> *Jesus said: "Look after the living one while you are living, lest you die and (find) you(rselves) powerless (when) you seek to see him."*

If only mankind could understand the urgency of renouncing the things of the world and seeking the salvific liberation no-one will provide for their soul but themselves, they would not hesitate to go through any length of trouble (see Logion 58). We established that the "living one" is the eidolon of the soul (see Logion 15), subsequently becoming her savior twin when we turn our attention to the center of our own being to seek the counsel of our *syzygos*. This can only be done while we are alive physically because our savior is not a cosmic being descended from some mythological heavens but a living entity who abides in the innermost chamber of our heart. His temple is our own person, and when we die, we cannot find him anywhere else. We must remember, the mystical sovereignty is not a locality but a dimension of awareness. To avoid the separation of death (see Logion 61), the lifetime quest of the *pneumatici* is to ensure their soul is betrothed to her savior. Whosoever "looks after the living one" gives him substance, shape, breath, and ultimately liberation through the offering of one's soul. If we do not look for him, we miss his inspiration, guidance, and salvific intervention: the stunted *syzygos* then departs at the moment of death, leaving the soul behind. The soul who is not sealed to her divine companion remains forlorn as incorporeal, dispersed memories in the physical sphere. The mind that was once the soul's vehicle dissipates with the lifeless corpse. The abandoned soul would never behold the presence of the Beloved again but for another dream of the "I AM" in which at last she is attuned to the desire of her *syzygos*. The mystical, reciprocal pursuit is voiced exquisitely in a Mandaean gnostic hymn from the *Ginza Rba*:

> *From the place of light have I gone forth,*
> *from thee, bright habitation.*
> *I come to feel the hearts,*
> *to measure and try all minds,*

to see in whose heart I dwell,
in whose mind I repose.
Who thinks of me, of him I think:
who calls my name, his name I call.
Who prays my prayer from down below,
his prayer I pray from the place of light...
I came and found
the truthful and believing hearts.
When I was not dwelling among them,
yet my name was on their lips.
I took them and guided them up to the world of light...

—Quoted in The Gnostic Religion by Hans Jonas

The First Death (Biological) - Logion 60

(They) saw a Samaritan carrying a lamb (as he was) on the way to Judea. He said to his disciples: "That one ... the lamb?" They said to him: "So that he might kill it and eat it." He said to them: "He will not eat it while living; yet, when he kills it and it becomes a corpse (he will)." They said: "He cannot do any other way." He said to them: "You too, seek after a place for you(rselves) in a

repose, lest you become corpses and be eaten."

Life on Earth—organic life—feeds on death. Everything that lives depends for nourishment on something that dies. It is the immutable law of the physical universe, and our biological existence is no more than a recycling process. Yet there is an escape from this morbid condition: if we can lift the self-sustaining eternal essence to sovereignty, we can grow as an immortal, etherealized being. Our true home is the place of light (see Logion 50) where the soul of the chosen will be transported to find repose.

The Second Death (Spiritual) - Logion 61

Jesus said: "Of two lying on a bed, one will die, the other will live." Salome said: "Who are you man? While out of one, you climbed onto my bed and ate off my table." Jesus said to her: "I am he who exists out of he who is equal (alt. 'sameness,' or 'undivided'). I partake of my father."

"I am your disciple."

"Because of this, I say, when he comes to be destroyed, he will be filled

> *with light; when, however, he comes to*
> *be divided, he will be full of darkness."*

In this cryptic oracular saying, Thomas returns to the motif of the monad (see Logia 22, 23) to expound the spiritual death of those who remain "divided."

Of the two lying on the bed—implicitly Jesus and Salome—Salome only will die physically because she is human while Jesus represents the living eidolon. She will also die the spiritual death (be full of darkness), which is the permanent separation of the soul from the *syzygos* (see Logion 59) at the moment of biological death. If, however, she is "destroyed," which in context can be understood as no longer divided (because that which was causing the division has been removed), she will be filled with light and find repose in the place of light (see logia 24, 50, and 83). In other words, it is the state of being divided that must be destroyed. The idea is supported by the fact the Greek name "Salome" is most likely derived from the Hebrew *shalem*, which means "complete," "whole" or "unbroken."

On one level, then, Salome is the disciple who must find the living one while she is alive (Logion 59) and mend the division of the divine essence within herself lest she be filled with darkness (see also Logion 24).

On the other hand, Salome here is yet another allegorical character who represents the soul. She must find her likeness in the living eidolon and become an undivided monad with her divine companion represented by Jesus who is resting next to her on the bed.

Beyond the Veil - Logion 62

> *Jesus said: "I tell my mysteries to [those who are worthy of my] mysteries. Do not let your left hand know that which your right hand will do."*

Jesus the living is the personification of he who imparts a hierophantic knowledge from within the vaulted chamber of one's own heart, and not between the walls of churches, temples, mosques, or synagogues. To find the mysteries, one needs to bypass the mind behind which they are hidden as if behind a veil. The natural organ of cognition mostly impedes our ability to comprehend the numinous. When we do not let our left hand be aware of what our right hand is doing, we effectively move toward a new form of cognition, a numinous insight (see also Logion 26) that lifts the backdrop off the stage of our mind.

The right hand also symbolizes the right path as suggested in George Wither's aphorism:

> *The Right-hand way, is Vertues Path,*
> *Though rugged Passages it hath.*
>
> ...
>
> *Though the Left-hand way, more smoothness hath,*

Let us goe forward, in the Right-hand-path.

* * *

A few occult organizations still use in their secret rituals (which are the corrupted remnants of ancient initiations into the mystery cults) a veil through which the initiate is being pulled by his right hand. The veil symbolizes the separation between the dark sublunar world of matter and an empyrean realm of light. It is also a reminder that sacred knowledge should often be protected (veiled) from the vulgar and the mundane, and saved for those who are who are worthy of the mysteries.

The right-hand path to the mysteries is for the righteous only to follow. In the 6th century BCE, Parmenides of Elea wrote a distinctively telestic poem describing the passage of an initiate from the vulgar world of the mortals to the realm of the gods:

> *... they brought me and set me <u>on the renowned Way of the goddess, who with her own hands conducts the man who knows through all things.</u> ... maidens showed the way. And the axle, glowing in the socket -*
>
> *for it was urged round by the whirling wheels at each*
>
> *end - gave forth a sound as of a pipe, when the daughters of the*
>
> *Sun, hasting to convey me into the light, threw back their veils*

from off their faces and left the abode of Night.

There are the gates of the ways of Night and Day, fitted

above with a lintel and below with a threshold of stone. They

themselves, high in the air, are closed by mighty doors, and

Avenging Justice keeps the keys that open them. Her did

the maidens entreat with gentle words and skillfully persuade

to unfasten without demur the bolted bars from the gates.

Then, when the doors were thrown back,

they disclosed a wide opening, when their brazen

hinges swung backwards in the

sockets fastened with rivets and nails. Straight through them,

on the broad way, did the maidens guide the horses and the car,

and <u>the goddess greeted me kindly, and took my right hand</u>

<u>in hers, and spake to me these words: -</u>

<u>Welcome, noble youth, that comest to my abode.</u>

(Emphases are mine.)

—John Burnet, Poem of Parmenides, English translation, 1892.

The Folly of Materialism - Logion 63

> *Jesus said: "There was a man of wealth who had many riches. He said: 'I will use my riches to sow, reap, plant, and to fill my treasure-house with fruit, so that I will not need anything.' These thoughts he had in his mind (alt. 'in his heart'); and in the present night, he died. He who has an ear to lend, let him listen."*

Little spiritual discernment is needed to understand the implications of this Logion. The message here—for once devoid of hidden subtext—is urgently conveyed to anyone who has an ear to lend: our engrossment with materialism is dire foolishness.

A man accumulates all he thinks he might need in life only to die the same day he completes his task. That is the irony of lives spent in preparation for hypothetical needs without a care for death who might come unannounced and swiftly. The ruling elite of the Etruscans, the Celts, and the Vikings, and the potentates of the ancient Chinese and Egyptian dynasties were entombed surrounded by their earthly possessions in a vain hope to perpetuate their privileged status in the afterlife. The modern individual may scoff at such poor spiritual foresight and awareness, but he is hardly more enlightened than his predecessors.

In our days, we simply ignore our impending demise and give ourselves entirely to the "pursuit of happiness" (the most inventive euphemism ever concocted for our obsession with property and the accumulation of the useless). Our "needs" are constantly pushed farther so that there is no possibility of fulfilling them: a blind intent that is the basis for industrial societies epitomized in capitalist America by its underpinning middle-class.

In his essay On the Vanity of Existence, the philosopher Arthur Schopenhauer remarks:

> *How insatiable a creature is man! Every satisfaction he attains lays the seeds of some new desire, so that there is no end to the wishes of each individual will.*

Crass materialism was made acceptable under the guise of an ideal to which we attached many values (including religious ones), but we are fooling ourselves: we left in the distant past our legitimate yearning for comfort and rushed headlong in a greedy chase after persistently receding aims. Oblivious to its annihilating power, we revel in the insatiability that devours us.

The rich man in Thomas' story uses his money to increase profits. Our descent in the bottomless ravine of greed begins the moment we seek to multiply gains beyond the requirements of our well-being. Tragically, we cannot discern the lies we are telling ourselves, and each step we believe is taking us closer to achieving our goal of "happiness" is in reality leading us away from the richness of the mystical sovereignty. And every new generation is both victim and perpetrator of the conditions that force us to run a race for illusory reward.

Mammon - Logion 64

Jesus said: "A man was having visitors and, when he had prepared the dinner, he sent his servant to call the visitors. He went to the first (and) said to him: 'My lord calls you.' He answered: 'I have money for traders who are coming tonight. I will go and place orders with them. I ask to be excused from the dinner.' He went to another one (and) said to him: 'My lord calls you.' He answered: 'I bought a house, and I am required for the day; I cannot ease off.' He went to another one (and) said to him: 'My lord calls you.' He answered: 'My friend is getting married, and I am the one who is making the dinner; I cannot come. I ask to be excused from the dinner.' He went to another one (and) said to him: 'My lord calls you.' He answered: 'I bought a farm, and I am going to

> *collect the taxes; I cannot come. I ask to be excused.' The servant came back (and) told his lord: 'Those you called to the dinner have excused themselves.' The lord told his servant: 'Go to the roads on the outskirts; bring those you may find so that they may dine.' The buyers and the trade[rs will] not [enter] the places of my father."*

Logion 64 does not shine by virtue of conciseness, and its meaning is more effectively conveyed in the gospel of Matthew:

> *No man can serve two masters: for either he will hate the one, and love the other; or else he will hold to the one, and despise the other. Ye cannot serve God and mammon.*
>
> —Matthew 6:24

The parable of the dinner guests broadens the impact of Logion 63. Are we the invitees who decline the invitation to eat at the table of the lord (our *syzygos*) because we are too busy with worldly concerns?

Our imprisonment in materiality is not just figurative: our divine essence is literally a prisoner of the physical world, and the walls of our materialistic donjon will not tumble unless we surrender to the living eidolon within ourselves. Yet, we are generally more preoccupied with our daily routines and earthly matters than we are interested in liberating our soul from physicality. Worse yet is the fate of those whose life is defined by financial success: the "buyers and traders" who are lured in the arms of mammon and miss the gates to the empyrean of the blessed. As the philosopher Georges Bernanos tells it:

> *Spiritual values will never be restored as long as profit is honored, whereas it should only be tolerated and controlled.*

Kill the Mind - Logion 65

> *He said: "A [...] man had a vineyard. He gave it to tenants so they might work on it (while) he would take the fruit of their labor. He sent his servant so that the tenants should give him the fruit of the vineyard. They grabbed his servant (and) beat him, nearly killing him. The servant went to tell his lord. His lord said that perhaps he did not know them. He sent another servant; the tenants beat that one (too). Then the master sent his son, saying that perhaps they would be ashamed before him, (he being his) son.' The tenants seized him and killed him because they knew he was the heir of the vineyard. He who has an ear to lend, let him listen."*

To understand the troubling parable in this Logion, one must think outside the paradigms we have been conditioned to accept. Readers will most certainly assume that the owner of the vineyard is a good man cheated and wronged by ingrate, evil tenants. Some will instantly make connections with the Christian myth of the Son of God sent by the Father to redeem the same men who would kill him. However, nowhere in the writings of Thomas can we find the concept of a redeemer son of God who suffers in Gethsemane, is crucified, and resurrected to save mankind from sin and death. In Thomas, the father and son figures are not mythical but allegorical. We should remember the warning of Logion 2 and be prepared for troubling truths: the hidden words of Thomas will not reinforce our preconceptions but invite us instead to turn our mental process upside down.

Logia 21 and 65 have a similar meaning, and we can use the former to interpret the latter.

The owner of the vineyard does not let his tenants enjoy the fruit of their labor; he wants to "collect" it for himself. He is not a good person, but the allegorical portrayal of the demiurge, the false god and mythical leader of the archons. The fruits (the souls) of the vineyard (the physical world) are at the center of a struggle for hegemony. To escape the confines of physicality, the savior twin needs to release the soul from the physical world. The lord of the vineyard and his servants (the demiurge and the archons) also covet the soul for their survival because she is the memories from which they derive their sense of identity (see Logion 21 and Appendix 2). They will do everything in their power to prevent the eloping of the soul with her savior twin.

The sharecroppers are the *pneumatici* (see Logion 73) who must take care their soul is surrendered to her legitimate heir (†). They resist the servants trying to dispossess them until the master sends his son (††). Who is this "son," the last card in the hand of the demiurge? He is our mind or natural self, the ultimate creation arising from matter, to which we owe the memories that shape our soul (†††). The mind, our ally throughout biological evolution, turns into an enemy in the evolution of consciousness. We ought to suppress the mind to let out the authentic Self in the same way a space rocket discards its booster to reach the stars. The mind that seeks to outlast its usefulness is not who we are, only the temporary vehicle of the anamnesis from which comes our individuality. Our true identity lies beyond the mind; it is the soul and her savior twin conjoined as a twy-formed god, the eternal "I am."

—

† Remember from Logion 21 that the children—the souls of the *pneumatici*—did not own the field on which they dwelled, just as the tenants do not own the vineyard.

†† The act of sending his unique son to certain harm without hesitation, just to recover his land, shows the selfish and cruel nature of the master and owner of the vineyard.

††† It is interesting here to draw a parallel between the father (demiurge/matter) and son (natural self/mind) of the vineyard allegory with the father ("I AM") and son (the soul) in Logion 15.

The Cornerstone of Life - Logion 66

> *Jesus said: "Show me the one stone those who build rejected; it is the cornerstone."*

The cornerstone of biological life is pneuma manifested as the psychic thrust that sustains all living things. The cornerstone of life eternal—the mystical sovereignty—is the savior twin who is the evolutionary magnum opus of the pneuma entrapped in matter. The builders who reject the cornerstone are the *hylici*, and to some extent the *psychici* who do not understand the multifaceted, changing nature of pneuma throughout its evolutionary metamorphoses and manifestations. They discard the notion of a psychic thrust pervading the field of reality in favor of a cosmic god, or the laws of physics.

Self-Deficiency - Logion 67

> *Jesus said: "He who knows everything, if he needs himself, he lacks the place entirely."*

The literal reading of the Coptic version of this saying is so obscure, it can only be interpreted, and interpretations with vastly differing meanings abound (†). The underlying idea can be clarified with the help of Logion 39, which tells us that the Pharisees and the scribes—presumably, those who claim to know everything—take and hide the keys of knowledge and yet do not "go in." In other words, they do not enter the place of light (Logion 50) and repose (Logion 90) that is the mystical sovereignty, in spite of all they know or think they know. And the reason is that a thorough knowledge is not a sufficient criterion of salvation when we persistently yield to the demands of a false self:

- If we cling to our natural self (need ourselves) with that which defines us in the world, we fail to recognize the living eidolon within who would lead us to the place where he is (see Logion 24).
- If we know ourselves (see Logion 3), we understand our dyadic, soul-*syzygos* nature. And the transformative experience of the soul reaching for her savior twin (the higher Self) is that which takes us to the gates of mystical sovereignty within.

—

† This should not surprise us: Thomas warned us the words he recorded were "veiled" (Logion 0). Since an understanding of the veiled words is the prerequisite to eternal life (Logion 1), we can expect the logia to lend themselves to extensive cogitations.

The Persecution of the World - Logion 68

> *Jesus said: "Blessed are you when they hate you and persecute you, and no place is found where they (can) persecute you within."*

We run into the same difficulty in making sense of this saying as we did for the previous one. In Logion 68, however, the translators find a ground of agreement because, curiously, they all elide one key word from the Coptic text: "within" ("in him"). "Place," and "within" are the key words (†) that help us elucidate this mysterious meditation.

At first glance, this Logion recalls Matthew 5:10, which is part of the "Beatitudes" in the Christian canon. Although the similarity is obvious, the difference is notable. The "Beatitudes" are mostly outwardly oriented: the promised blessings rest on the disciples' response to adversity. In Thomas however, the disciple is blessed through internal resolution of his existential struggle.

The historical persecutions of the early Christians came about as the result of their overt, often fanatical opposition to the social order and religious ideals of their time. The Gnostics, on the other hand, were indifferent to the social order and state-sanctioned cults whether or not they approved of them: their quest unfolded in the vaulted chamber of their own heart, and within the confines of their mind. The seeker of gnosis is less likely to be persecuted in the world if he is not involved with the world.

The evangelist Matthew appears to encourage undergoing tribulations for the sake of a disconcerting display of faith:

> *Blessed are they which are persecuted for righteousness' sake: for theirs is the kingdom of heaven.*
>
> *Blessed are ye, when men shall revile you, and persecute you, and shall say all manner of evil against you falsely, for my sake.*
>
> *Rejoice, and be exceeding glad: for great is your reward in heaven: for so persecuted they the prophets which were before you.*
>
> —Matthew 5:10-12

What sort of demented father wants to see his children suffer? Based on Matthew's claims, the Christians developed a sadomasochist theurgy of suffering, deliberately courting hate and persecution to achieve glory. In the middle-ages, monks pushed the psychosis even farther with the practice of self-inflicted harm and pain to share in the sufferings of Christ and grow nearer to their insane god. Thomas never says it is saintly or desirable to suffer for any god or religion. The blessing of the countless anonymous individuals who, for unwarranted reason, suffer distress and trauma comes from the realization that the lower sphere of existence will always be the domain of cruelty, violence, and injustice.

The gospel of Thomas ushers us instead to the true home of the soul where only joy, beauty, and harmony abide.

The mystical sovereignty that is the "place within" cannot be found by either the torturer or the victim in the sensible world where hate and persecution occur, because it belongs to the suprasensible realm of the innermost, where it remains untouched by suffering.

—

† Incidentally, key words are often found in two or three sequential logia, making it safe to infer they are used with the same intent of meaning.

Spiritual Hunger - Logion 69

> *Jesus said: "Blessed are they who have been persecuted in their heart (alt. 'in their mind'); they know the father in truth. Blessed are they who are hungry, so they may satisfy the belly of he who desires."*

The saying clarifies and expand on Logion 68 with a metaphor. Verse 1 reprises the idea of those who are blessed when persecuted because they recognize that the world of suffering is irredeemable. They seek the place within where they can know the father who cannot be found on the sensible plane (the reason the gnostics called him the "invisible father").

The 12th century Cathars understood the bread mentioned in the scriptures as *supersubstantial*. It was not the bread that satisfies physical hunger, let alone the flesh of Christ, but the spiritual nourishment of those who recognize the true father. That is the meaning of verse 2 in the saying. The "hunger" of which Logion 69 is speaking is not the need for solid nutriment but a spiritual appetence, an urge even more vital for the earnest seeker to satisfy. And the inner revelations flowing from the living eidolon are the only satisfying nourishment for those who are spiritually famished.

The Birth of the Savior - Logion 70

> *Jesus said: "When you give birth to the one in yourselves, he who is in you will save you. If you do not have him in [you], he whom you do not have in you [will] kill you."*

Because the Coptic language attribute a gender to all things (as for instance the French language does) translator often use the English neutral when they read a reference to an inanimate subject. In Logion 70, however, it does actually make sense to keep the masculine pronoun with the understanding it stands for the savior twin.

In this saying then, we continue to explore the recesses of our inner depths where the processes of etherealization occurs. If we were to take away only one verse from the gospel of Thomas for personal guidance, this could be the one. Indeed, this cryptic aphorism is the key to salvific freedom, and there is no metaphysical door it cannot open.

The reality of everything we perceive can legitimately be called into question except the fact we are the agent of perception: the "I" within who observes the individual observer of the physical universe.

In Logion 70 we find the unambiguous declaration that salvation is not to be expected from outside means or vehicles: it comes from within. All the analogies, allegories, and the symbolism in the pithy sayings of Thomas are signposts pointing to "him whom we have within ourselves."

We saw that pneuma exhaled by the god-being transforms, develops, and travels through generations until that day it finds the receptive heart where it can dwell as a living presence (Logia 29, 59). It is the attention the *pneumatici* give to this expectation that allows a metamorphose to unfurl from the psychic thrust in man to the savior twin of the soul, arisen in the core of our being. Instead of prostituting herself to the world (see Logion 105), the soul must give birth to her living eidolon and become the liberator of the savior twin born to save her. However, if we do not have him within us, the soul remains alone. Without her eternal companion to wrest her away from the grip of matter, she is left behind when we die and the pneuma departs. Such is the spiritual, or second death (see Logion 61): "he whom we do not have within [will] kill us" us because, detached from the *syzygos*, the memories that shape the soul are bound to physicality. Our fragmented individuality is condemned to hover in the sensible world, phantom-like and without awareness.

In a fashion, the neo-Christians are right: salvation is easy and does consist in accepting a mythological being as our savior. Only, that being did not walk the earth and does not come from the sky; and we can only be born-again in him if he is first born in us.

The Demise of the House - Logion 71

> *Jesus said: "I will destroy [this] house,
> and no one will be able to [re]build it."*

We asserted that the "house" so often mentioned in Thomas (Logia 16, 21, 35, 48, 98) is not an edifice of stones, wood, and cement, but the body that houses the soul. The dualist has only disdain for the body of flesh and bones he regards as both a tomb for the divine essence, and a corpse bound to decay (unlike the pneuma that can never be destroyed). When the "I AM" exhales, it stirs the field of Apeiron, and the god-being dreams into manifestation the material world, and human existence with its appendant fleshy vehicle. The builder of the house and its destroyer are the primordial duality of man (see Logion 7). When the household abandon their temporary dwelling, the habitacle crumbles to dust. No one can build that house again: there is no resurrection of the physical body; eternal life is housed in a body of light (see Logia 83 and 84).

He Who Unites - Logion 72

> *[A man said to him]: "Speak to my brothers so they may divide the belongings of my father with me." He said to him this: "O man, who made me a divider?" He turned to his disciples (and) said to them: "Truly, am I to be a divider?"*

Once again, sadly, the disciples are more preoccupied by trivial matters than focused on giving birth to the savior within. They want a ruler who can arbitrate the conflicts of their petty lives. Yet, the living eidolon does not divide anything in the realm of the mortals but heals in the heart the diffluence of sempiternal Desire.

Desire divides itself to conquer itself and return self-reflecting into the plenitude (Logia 3 part I, 16, and 61). While men of the world, the—*hylici* and *psychici* alike—may be anxious to divide an estate, our true inheritance is the monad formed by the confluence of soul and *syzygos*.

The Harvest - Logion 73

> *Jesus said: "Indeed, the harvest is plentiful; however, the workers are*

> *few. Pray however to the Lord so he might send workers to the harvest."*

In the symbolic word choices of Thomas, the harvest is that time when the seed (parcels) of pneuma have developed and matured (see Logion 57). There are as many seeds as there are sentient beings on the planet, but only the truthful carry in his heart the fruit of the living eidolon. The harvest could be plentiful but for the scarcity of workers: the *pneumatici*, the chosen who are able to turn their soul into an agent of liberation for the savior twin. No one else, regardless of how "spiritual," religious, or morally good they might be, is fit to work at the harvest. Everyone could become a worker of salvation unto himself if only they understood they are both the harvesters and that which is harvested. The disciples have yet to pray for the knowledge they need and transform themselves into the artisans of their own salvific liberation.

The Living Water - Logion 74

> *He said: "Lord, there are many around the fountain, however, nothing (is) in the well."*

The ambiguity of the Coptic here lends two possible meanings to the saying in Thomas: either there is no water, or no one in the well. However, scholars quote the saying as it appears to have been use by the Ophites as well: "Why are there many around the well and no one in the well?"

The idea, then, is that we circle the place of the living water, we crowd its portal, but we do not cross its threshold. This is confirmed in the next saying, which makes use of a different metaphor for the same observation.

Regardless, the water from the well is the living water of which Jesus spoke in his conversation with a Samaritan woman in the Gospel of John (see John 4:10). The well symbolizes our own depths, and the water therein is the voice of the *syzygos* who leads on the path of gnosis those who are thirsty for the salvific knowledge. Much like Logion 73 before, Logion 74 is a reflection on how few are able (or willing) to reach out within for guidance and meaning. Some gather around the well but do not go inside to draw the water for themselves: they are the *psychici* who rely on the experiences, explanations, and directions of others to build their faith. The innermost of the others is dry, devoid of the flow of living water: such is the condition of the *hylici* who will not accept (or simply do not care for) the reality of a plane of existence beyond the world of senses.

The Bridal Chamber - Logion 75

> *Jesus said: "There are many standing at the door, but only those who are a monad will enter the place of marriage."*

In the mythological tale of Eros and Psyche the two protagonists respectively personify Desire and the soul. Desire is the primary cause at the origin of creation, and the sustainer of existence. Thus, in the ancient mysteries, Eros was recognized as Protogenos: the ferment of life; he who existed before the beginning and in whom all things originated. Desire is carried forth through pneuma, the self-sustaining, everlasting, moving force of reality. The myth tells us how Eros and Psyche were fated to an overwhelming, reciprocal passion. They begin their liaison in mysterious circumstances by meeting every night in the darkened bedchamber of a beautiful palace. At first Psyche cannot see who her inamorato is, but she uncovers his identity by lightening with her lamp (figuratively the guiding light of gnosis; see Logion 33) the alcove where they lie. After many tribulations Eros and Psyche's perseverance is rewarded with immortality; the child of their love is Hedone, meaning pleasure and delight. The classical theme of the lover and the beloved was at the core of the mystery cults that allegorized the mystical coupling (henosis) of the human soul with her creator. It is also the motif hidden in the imagery of the gospel of Thomas.

The souls of the *hylici* and *psychici* alike are standing outside the bridal chamber. They never open the door because they do not have the key (see Logion 39). The *pneumatici* are "made a monad": their soul is betrothed to her *syzygos* (Logion 23) because they have the keys of gnosis that open the door to the sacred room where the savior twin is waiting. In the secret garden of the heart, the soul knows her lover and becomes one with him.

The Pearl that Never Perishes - Logion 76

> *Jesus said: "The mystical sovereignty of the father can be compared to a trader with merchandise who found a pearl. The trader who was wise sold his merchandise to buy that single pearl for himself. "You, yourselves, seek this treasure that does not perish but endures, the place where no moth comes to eat, and no worm destroys."*

The traders in Thomas are those who concern themselves with material instead of spiritual wealth (see Logion 64). However, a wiser one soon recognizes the folly of his ways and abandons what he owns in favor of a single pearl. In esoteric, gnostic literature, the pearl is another recurring symbol for the parcel of pneuma, shining and beautiful, but a prisoner of its shell until found by the soul who cherishes her priceless acquisition. It is the only treasure that matters, the heavenly gift of the savior twin whose company endures for eternity when all that is earthly perishes and decays. Alternatively, in the context of the gospel of Thomas and its emphasis on salvific knowledge, the pearl can be understood as the keys of gnosis (see Logion 39) that lead to the one's savior twin.

Immanence, Transcendence, and Permanence - Logion 77

> Jesus said: "I am the light that is over all things. I am everything. Everything has come out from me and is in me.
> "Split a log; I am there. Lift the stone, and you will find me there."

The raison d'être of everything is the perpetuation of the "I AM" through an actualization of all things. And all things are actualized through the sempiternal Desire that comes out of the god-being—his sustaining intent—without ever depleting him (see Logion 15). The god-being abides forever while simultaneously in the process of becoming. Thus he is above everything and in all things. He is present in the substance of the wood and the stone, or in the heart of whom splits the wood and lifts the stone (†). This god of whom Thomas speaks, both immanent and transcendent, was also understood by his Hypsistarians contemporaries who described him with no less poetic sentiment:

> He is the Lord of all, self-originated, self-produced, ruling all things in some ineffable way, encompassing the heavens, spreading out the earth, riding on the waves of the sea; ... leading all

> *things towards the light and settling their fate in harmonious order.*

—Source: Catholic Encyclopedia, volume 7

We are constantly touching the divine. The mystical sovereignty, therefore, has no boundary: it is a dimension of awareness, a window from which we look inside or outside depending on where we stand. But from the point of view of the window itself there is no such distinction, as in and out are just artificial partitioning of the whole. (See also Logion 3).

—

† Interestingly, Jesus is generally thought to have been either a carpenter or a stonemason, which could have had a bearing on the choice of occupations mentioned in this saying.

The Desert within - Logion 78

> *Jesus said: "For what reason did you come outdoors? To see a reed moved by the wind? And to see a [man] wearing fine clothing, [like your] kings and the powerful ones? Upon them [are] fine [clothing] and they cannot know the truth."*

Because of the similarity of this logion with verses in Luke and Matthew, commentators on the Gospel of Thomas often think it must be referring to John the Baptist. But unlike the other evangelists, Thomas does not follow a narrative, and his sayings typically expand on each other. Whereas Logion 77 tells us the all-pervading psychic thrust of sempiternal Desire is in a split log or under a stone, Logion 78 notes that people seek for answers in all the wrong places: they are like someone looking for a well-dressed person, or a water reed in the middle of a deserted, parched land. This evocative image is followed by a warning not to trust the rulers and those in a position of authority who mainly mislead us despite the respectable facade they present. In the solitude of the silent desert within is where we find numinous direction. (See also Logia 52, 70).

The Mother of the Living One - Logion 79

A woman in the crowd said to him, "Blessed is the belly that bore you, and the breasts that nourished you." He said to [her]: "Blessed are those who have listened to the word of the father and kept it in truth. The days will come to be you will say this: 'Blessed is the belly that did not conceive and the breasts that did not give milk.'"

The dualist does not subscribe to the edict of multiplying and filling the earth, nor does he think it a blessing to procreate. From the demiurge, the false god who rules over the cosmos, come the encouragements to mankind's reproductive impulse as a subterfuge to trap parcels of pneuma in the realm of matter.

And, with the help of Logion 70, there is yet more esoteric meaning to uncover in Logion 79: "When you give birth to the one in yourself, he who is in you will save you." The soul (the individuality, or inner self) is the mother who gives birth—through her reflection in the innermost (see Logion 5)—without having to conceive or give milk, and the living eidolon is her son (in Logion 15: "he who was not born of the woman"). The soul is blessed because she is mother to her savior. This is allegorized in the Catholic dogma as the virgin birth of Jesus (the living eidolon) who was conceived in the womb of his mother Mary (representing the soul) through the spirit, without sexual encounter.

The Nature of the Body - Logion 80

> *Jesus said: "Whoever has known the world has found the body; but whoever has found the body, of him the world is not worthy."*

This logion is nearly identical to Logion 56 save for the word "body" substituted here for "corpse." Together, the two sayings play on the twofold nature of our corporal envelope and, by extension, of the world. On the one hand, the earthy abide is a tomb for the pneuma, a repulsive aggregation of particles of gross matter, the slowly decaying walls keeping our divine essence prisoner; on the other hand, the body of flesh and bones and the planet are also the temporary home of the soul (see Logion 71) and a temple for her deification: the house of the immanent and transcendent god (see Logion 77). Paradoxically, the world hampers the very psychic thrust that sustains its own life. Matter and flesh are not evil, they are the paradox of necessity.

Power and Wealth - Logion 81

> *Jesus said: "Whoever has become rich, let him become king, and he who has power, let him renounce (it)."*

In Thomas' philosophy, the power yielded by the rulers, and the wealth of the powerful belong to the realm of matter. Logion 63 tells us about the folly of the rich man, and Logion 78 explains that the kings and the powerful who wear fine clothing "cannot know the truth." In this light the meaning of the saying is revealed: money rules the world, and the rulers of the world are the rich. Anyone finding himself in such a mighty position should weight his priorities, as will be confirmed in Logion 110. One cannot serve God and mammon (see Logion 64). For the *pneumatici*, the physical plane has nothing of authentic value to offer. They must seek to be sovereign over the entirety (see Logion 2) through a knowledge of themselves, which is to be rich spiritually (see Logion 3, part II).

Keeping near the Fire - Logion 82

> *Jesus said: "He who is close to me is close to the fire, and he who is far from me is far from the mystical sovereignty."*

The *pneumatici* who turn to the living eidolon within can feel the intensity of the divine fire (Logion 10), the breath of the god-being that makes them spiritually alive in the world of the dead. Those who lack this inward focus (see Logion 67) lose numinous direction and move farther to ever finding the keys to the mystical sovereignty.

The Image and the Light - Logion 83

> *Jesus said: "The images are revealed to man, and the light within them is hidden in the image of the father's light. He will be revealed, and his image (will be) hidden by his light."*

The images "revealed to man" are those we perceive in the realm of matter: our perishable bodies of flesh and bones shown in the spectrum of light caught by the human eye. The hidden image of the father is the transcendent aspect ("the light that is over all things" - see Logion 77) of the god-being who remains in the place of light (see Logion 15). Because we are the children of the invisible father, our bodies are made in his image (see Logion 50) and carry his light (see Logion 24). The image of the soul reflected in the innermost is the that "of the father's light": the living eidolon who carries the divine light into or mortal envelopes (see Logion 50). Thus, the living eidolon reveals the father, but the image of the god-being himself remains hidden until we return to the realm of light and regain our divine likeness (see Logion 84 below).

The Robe of Glory – Logion 84

> *Jesus said: "When you behold your likeness, you rejoice. However, when you behold your images that come to be at your beginning—they do not die nor are they revealed—how much will you bear?"*

When we "behold our likeness," we will be in the presence of the savior twin, rejoicing in the etherealized body that will be the next vehicle of our soul (see Logion 22). When the soul and her *syzygos* become a monad, the twy-formed god will re-enter the mystical sovereignty whence he came, recovering the eternal image the "I AM" leaves behind when we descend into the physical world.

The recovery of our glorious likeness is poetically described at the end of the "Hymn of the Robe of Glory," an ancient allegory also attributed to Thomas. The robe symbolizes the transcendent body of light (see Logion 22). It is a lengthy quote worth reproducing here for its sheer lyrical beauty and because it recalls many motifs we have uncovered in the gospel of Thomas:

> *My Glorious Robe that I'd stripped off,*
> *And my Mantle with which it was covered,*
> *Down from the Heights of Hyrcania,*
> *Thither my Parents (1) did send me,*
> *By the hands of their Treasure-dispensers*
> *Who trustworthy were with it trusted.*
> *Without my recalling its fashion, –*
> *In the House (2) of my Father my childhood (3) had left it, –*
> *At once, as soon as I saw it,*
> *The Glory looked like my own self (4).*
> *XVI.*
> *I saw it in all of me,*
> *And saw me all in [all of] it (5), –*
> *That we were twain in distinction,*
> *And yet again one in one likeness (6).*
> *I saw, too, the Treasurers also,*
> *Who unto me had down-brought it,*
> *Were twain [and yet] of one likeness (6);*
> *For one Sign of the King was upon them –*
> *Who through them restored me the Glory,*
> *The Pledge of my Kingship [?].*
> *XVII.*

The Glorious Robe all-bespangled
With sparkling splendour of colours:
With Gold and also with Beryls,
Chalcedonies, iris-hued [Opals?],
With Sards of varying colours.
To match its grandeur [?], moreover, it had been completed:
With adamantine jewels
All of its seams were off-fastened.
[Moreover] the King of Kings' Image **(7)**
Was depicted entirely all o'er it;
And as with Sapphires above
Was it wrought in a motley of colour.
XVIII.
I saw that moreover all o'er it
The motions of gnosis abounding;
I saw it further was making
Ready as though for to speak.
I heard the sound of its Music
Which it whispered as it descended [?]:
"Behold him the active in deeds!
For whom I was reared with my Father;
"I too have felt in myself
How that with his works waxed my stature."
XIX.
And [now] with its Kingly motions
Was it pouring itself out towards me,
And made haste in the hands of its Givers,

That I might [take and] receive it.
And me, too, my love urged forward
To run for to meet it, to take it.
And I stretched myself forth to receive it;
With its beauty of colour I decked me,
And my Mantle of sparkling colours
I wrapped entirely all o'er me.
XX.
I clothed me therewith, and ascended
To the Gate of Greeting and Homage.
I bowed my head and did homage
To the Glory of Him who had sent it,
Whose commands I [now] had accomplished,
And who had, too, done what He'd promised.
[And there] at the Gate of His House-sons
I mingled myself with His Princes;
For He had received me with gladness,
And I was with Him in His Kingdom;

—From the Hymn of Judas Thomas the Apostle in the Country of the Indians, translated by G.R.S. Mead.

Notes:

(1) The twy-formed god – see Logion 18.

(2) The place of light – see Logion 59.

(3) The descent into the physical world – see for instance Logia 18 and 29.

(4) The living eidolon or image of the soul – see for instance Logia 5 and 52.

(5) This verse shows that the "robe" is also a transcendent body.

(6) The soul and her savior twin – see Logion 22.

(7) The image of the father hidden in the place of light.

The Demiurge's Creation - Logion 85

> *Jesus said: "Adam came into being out of a great power and great wealth, and he did not become worthy of you. Had he been worthy, [he would not have tasted] death."*

Logion 85 is related to Logion 56 and has similar implications. Adam was the original man, the representative of humankind with a carnal body of the same nature as the sphere he was commanded to rule and subdue (abuse). The demiurge created Adam as a coarse image of clay. The false god of "great power and great wealth" (we learned in Logion 81 that wealth and power define the rulers of the world) then insufflated—according to gnostic tradition—a captured parcel of pneuma into his physical body to make him a "living being" (see Genesis 2:7). But Adam never truly lived. He was just the first creature to be entombed in matter (see Logion 11), walking its surface only temporarily, until the corpse, no longer sustained by the essence it kept captive, perishes and decays. Adam was also spiritually dead because he returned to the worship of the false god after having abandoned the wisdom he received from the enlightened serpent in the garden of Eden. Adam spent the rest of his life as a slave of the pretender god without realizing he was no mere servant but the eternal "I AM" prisoner in the cosmos. The begetter of mankind did not become worthy of the chosen (see Logia 9 and 23), the few of his children who understand the gnosis of the living eidolon.

The Home of the Living One - Logion 86

> Jesus said: "[The foxes have their dens] and the birds have their nests, but the son of man does not have a place to lay his head and rest."

The "son of man" is the living eidolon because he is fathered by those who "give birth to the one in themselves" (see Logion 70). The soul is his mother (see Logion 79). He is called "son of a harlot" in Logion 105 by reason of his affiliation to the realm of matter where the soul wanders miserably. But the living eidolon is not of this world and his permanent home is not here in the sublunar realm. He comes from the "place of light" and will return to the light (see Logion 50) with his betrothed, the soul. Unlike the animals who make their dwellings on Earth, the eternal crosses this plane as a mere passerby (see Logion 42).

The Two Bodies - Logion 87

> *Jesus said: "Miserable is the body that clings to a body, and miserable is the soul that clings to both."*

The interpretation of this Logion can be first inferred from Logia 7 and 11, which allude to the horrifying condition of man on earth, forced to sustain his life by eating the flesh on carcasses. Furthermore, decay is what makes biological life possible. The curse on Adam was not a condemnation to die but a sentencing to exist in a state conditioned by death. When Adam and Eve discovered they were naked in the garden of Eden, they sewed together fig leaves to make loincloths. Admittedly, their tailoring skills may not have been very developed, but with the help of a god they could have learned to use cotton or other natural fibers, you would think. The demiurge had other plans though: he preferred to cover "his children" with the flayed skin (†) of dead animals. Thenceforth heir forms would be enveloped in death (see Genesis 3:21). Next, the god of decay would demand blood sacrifices. Fruits and grains would not suffice, it had to be a lamb sliced alive on an altar (see Genesis 4:4). How "miserable" indeed is the soul for depending on the body in the realm of death.

Furthermore, logion 80 informs us that "whoever has known the world has found the body. The body that clings to the body, then, is the man incapable of renouncing the appeal of the material world: his "miserable" body perishes and decays in the world with which it shares the same substance; his miserable soul who "clings to both" is not released from her carnal envelope and dies with it on the physical plane.

We have already made a distinction in Logia 83 and 84 between the body of gross matter and the heavenly body of light, which nevertheless are in the same image, and a reflection of each other. The eternal body of light is born in the prison of the physical body when the soul seeks her image in the depth. The soul (the memories of one's lifetime) too arises in the living tissues on which it depends for a season. At the time of death, the anamneses of the chosen are transferred to the body of light to etherealize one's individuality and preserve it eternally in the person of the twy-formed god. A soul cannot stand on its own, and the memories of those who have not followed their savior twin will disperse in matter.

* * *

The Mormon Church (a creed fostered by the archons for their own glorification and the advancement of their designs) has a set of scriptures—the Book of Moses—that promulgates animal sacrifice as a law (see Moses 5:5) revealed to Adam by Elohim, the cosmic god of flesh and bones. The Mormons also believe they will receive a corporeal exaltation (they think of the spirit as a lacking, inferior condition) on a renewed Earth brought into the proximity of the planet where the Heavenly, or Celestial

Father lives. The whole "LDS" archonic mythology adds weight to the laments of Thomas. Not faring better, the Jehovah's Witnesses anticipate for themselves a literal resurrection in human forms, with the same human body they had at the moment of death. [Pardon me for not being interested!]

—

† Of particular interest is the contrast between the skin of animals—a clear allusion to the body of flesh covering our mortal souls on Earth—and the robe of glory promised to the immortal soul described in the *Hymn of Thomas* (quoted in Logion 84).

Godspel - Logion 88

> *Jesus said: "The angels and the prophets will come to you, and they will give you those things you have. You will give them those things and tell yourselves: 'When will they come and take that which is theirs?'"*

The angels—who were mere foot messengers before they acquired wings; see for instance Genesis 18: 1-5—and the prophets are the representatives of revealed religion (†), part of an extensive mythological corpus that comes with ossified teachings, dogma, precepts, rules, and commandments. These outsiders to the inner temple impose themselves with a knowledge hardly worth the attention of the *pneumatici* whose well of wisdom is the depth of their own being. There is no truth the *gnostici* do not already hold within themselves, and they should be the ones instructing would-be messengers, winged or not! Emissaries and missionaries insist on spreading the words they have received from others when they should take the time to claim their own truth in the innermost. What is the precious truth, the pearl of wisdom (see Logia 76, 93) everyone already possesses as a hidden treasure? The answer was given in Logion 70: "he who is in you"—the keeper salvific knowledge—"will save you."

—

† For instance, the angels Gabriel and Moroni had a pivotal role in the foundation of Islam and Mormonism respectively.

Empty Rituals - Logion 89

> *Jesus said: "Why do you wash the outside of the cup? Do you not understand that whoever created the inside is also he who created the outside?"*

The artisan who crafted the cup made both its outside and inside. Likewise, the maker of the cosmos created everything in it. He is not the god of truth and light, but the demiurge, the false god who rules over matter. Rituals specifically intended for purity are therefore moot. They cannot do anything when apply to parts of a whole that is gross and impure. No protocol can make matter pure. What is pure does not need purification but distillation: our true essence belongs elsewhere.

If we take the cup to symbolize the human body, the saying would then apply to baptism and ritual bathing that cannot purify or wash away anything, especially our sins that originate in a human nature derived from the demiurge's own flaws and weakness.

The Yoke of the Living One - Logion 90

> *Jesus said: "Come to me, because my yoke is easy and my sovereignty is gentle, and you will find repose."*

When we follow or savior twin, we are refreshed by the living water Jesus promised to the Samaritan woman (see John 4: 10-14). The Gospel of John was dear to the Gnostics and Cathars alike because of its mystagogic bent and the way it lends itself to esoteric interpretation. Out of the four evangelists, only John recounts the meeting at the well:

> *But the hour cometh, and now is, when the true worshippers shall worship the Father in spirit and in truth: for the Father seeketh such to worship him. God is a Spirit: and they that worship him must worship him in spirit and in truth.*
>
> —John 4:23-24

To "worship him in spirit and in truth" is the yoke and requirement of the living eidolon—the "God [who] is a Spirit" (see Logion 15): there is no demand for moral conduct, no commandment, adhesion to creeds, work of faith, church attendance, abnegation, asceticism, religious study, spiritual exercise, or discipline. One must worship in spirit and truth, and that is all.

Reading the Present - Logion 91

> They said to him: "Tell us who you are so that we may believe in you." He said to them: "You read the face of the sky and the earth, and he who was in your presence you do not know, and you do not know [how] to read the present."

The disciples again are characteristically obtuse. Instead of choosing the easy yoke and gentle sovereignty of the living eidolon (see Logion 90), they ask for a figurehead to tell them what to do and what to think. Those who do not know how to worship in spirit and truth need someone in whom to believe, who will promise them earthly blessings and heavenly rewards. The disciples want a flesh-and-blood Jesus to lead them, and they cannot sense the constant companion within (see for instance Logion 52). They trust their physical eyes; they read patterns and make predictions; but they do not have the numinous sight to discern that which is permanent (see also Logion 77): the mystical sovereignty is not to come, it is already here; salvific liberation is not in the future, it is now.

Asking the Right Questions - Logion 92

> *Jesus said: "Seek and you will find. Yet, the things you asked me about in days past, I did not tell you. Now, it pleases me to tell you, but you seek them not."*

What do we really mean when we claim to be a seeker of the truth, or that we are looking for answers? When you engage in conversations with people who purport to be genuinely interested in knowing what is true, you soon discover their openness is not limitless. They set stiff markers on borders they will not cross or expand. Their search is within a paradigm broad enough to give them the illusion they are leaving behind their comfort zone (and more often than not to let them brag about what they know) but, in reality, they are unwilling to be troubled (see Logion 2), and they prefer to tell than to listen.

Logion 92 is a remonstrance to the disciples who either ask perpetually the wrong questions (†)—to which they get no answer—or are not honestly ready to be told what they would not bear.

—

† For instance, in Logia 6, 18, 37, and 51, the disciples are not given direct replies to their queries but hints to what they should have been asking instead.

Sparing the Sacred Knowledge - Logion 93

> *"Do not give that which is holy to the dogs lest they throw those things unto the dung heap. Do not throw pearls [to] the swine lest they make it [...]"*

Although the end of this Logion is defective, we can safely assume nothing good is happening to the pearls.

In context (see Logion 39), that which is holy and precious is the salvific knowledge. We saw that self-assured seekers often ask the wrong questions or are not ready for forthright answers. Worse yet, people rarely appreciate the worth of guidance given to them unconditionally. Oddly, they prefer difficulty, a price to pay, the allure of mystery, or the aura of authority as a cachet of authenticity. They want the elitist feeling and sense of superiority that easily come with practicing something of which others are not cognizant. They value the source more than the information itself and are easily impressed by exotic concoctions, expensive seminars, pretentious books, pseudo-secrecy, the veneer of antiquity, or the charisma of orators. Anyone who has frequented online forums knows firsthand the fervor of self-absorbed participants who are mostly interested in expounding the vastness of their erudition or enlightenment.

We need to remember that sharing gnosis is not a mandate to squander precious knowledge throughout the entire world, but a responsibility to inspire the truthful hearts (see Logia 31, 32 and 33).

The Promise - Logion - 94

> *Jesus [said]: "He who seeks will find; [and he who calls] in, it will be opened to him."*

Logion 94 refers us once more (see also Logion 92) to the primary promise of the gospel of Thomas stated in Logion 2. If we never stop looking, our persistence will be rewarded beyond expectations. This is the assurance, both simple and momentous, offered by the living eidolon. Its lack of flourish is perhaps the reason few find it appealing (see Logion 93). The *psychici* would rather follow the masses and go where the trends lead; the *pneumatici* know the sacred knowledge is found within. Therefore, the only door at which we should knock is the door of our innermost.

The Stumbling Block - Logion 95

> *[Jesus said]: "If you have money, do not lend it at interest. Rather, give [it*

> *to] him from whom [you] will not get it back."*

In the material world (especially the societies that encourage a capitalist system), one cannot be content with his fortune unless he makes it grow. Sadly, few of the most fortunate are aware that with each increase of wealth they build an ever-rising wall separating them from the treasure that does not perish (see Logion 76). Why do the rich never stop accumulating goods and money beyond reasonable needs? Whatever reasons they may put forward, they would do well to follow the admonition of Logion 95 because their obsession leads them away from the "places of the father" (see Logia 64 and 81).

The Growth of the Mystical Sovereignty - Logion 96

> *Jesus [said]: "The mystical sovereignty of the father can be compared to a woman (who) took a little bit of leaven that she [hid] in dough. She made it (into) large (loaves of) bread. He who has an ear to lend, let [him] listen"*

In Logion 20, the disciples asked to what the kingdom of heaven could be compared. How can you describe what is unfathomable for the natural senses or to the human organ of cognition? To answer, Thomas used the imaginative picture of a small seed growing into a tree where the birds could take shelter. In Logion 96, the invisible mystical sovereignty of the father is likened not to something insignificant that has the inherent power to grow larger, but to that which is the cause of expansion. Seeds and leaven are symbols of the parcels of pneuma fallen into matter, igniting the rise of the mystical sovereignty (as the yeast makes the bread rise) in the heart of the truthful. A single spark develops into a blazing fire (see Logion 10), indicating that the mystical sovereignty is not a place but the apotheosis of the psychic thrust, and the crest of the tide of Apeiron (see Logion 3).

The Prophecy - Logion 97

> *Jesus said: "The mystical sovereignty of the [father can be] compared to a woman carrying a [jar] full of meal. She was walking (down) [a] distant road (when) the jar's handle broke; the meal spilled out behind her on the road. She did not know (that) to be (so) (and) did not realize the problem. When she arrived home, she put the jar down (and) found it to be empty."*

Logion 97 stands apart from the rest of the sayings as a daring prediction for the 114 Logia in the gospel of Thomas.

Through the blind agency of the woman in this parable, the salvific knowledge (the meal represents the spiritual nourishment; see Logion 69) is spread in the open to guide the souls of men and help them reach the invisible mystical sovereignty of the father. So, having travelled through the long road of time, Fate reaches her destination to see that the wisdom she was carrying in the jar had "spilled out behind her on the road." Here is a cue to understand the parable: whereas everyone keeps wondering about the meaning of the empty jar, nobody asks what happened to the meal.

In 1945, an Egyptian farmer and his brothers found the Gospel of Thomas and other manuscripts sealed in an earthenware jar hidden in a cave. The farmer broke the container and removed its content, whereupon leaving the broken jar empty. Subsequently, the books were dispersed and sold on the black market before being painstakingly gathered again; the sacred knowledge they contained was spread around the entire world for the benefits of all souls.

Killing the Powerful One - Logion 98

> *Jesus said: "The mystical sovereignty of the father can be compared to a man who wanted to kill a powerful man. He drew his sword in his house and drove it into the wall so that he might know*

> *for himself his hand would be strong.*
> *Then he slew the powerful one."*

A murdering plot seems like an odd comparison to describe the invisible mystical sovereignty of the father, unless salvific liberation did depend on the death of someone powerful. We know from Logion 85 that the creation is overseen by the demiurge, the mythological embodiment of the universe, the god-figure worshiped by humankind since the days of Adam. In that aspect, he is also the governor of the archons whose permanent home is the cosmos. The powerful one must be killed to prevent the archons from interfering with the coupling of the soul and her savior twin, which is the means of their liberation from matter. Once again, the "house" figuratively stands for our body, both a dwelling for the soul and her prison (see Logion 71). The gospel of Thomas then, details our escape plan and gives us a weapon: the sword of sacred knowledge (see Logion 16) we drive through the walls of physicality to evade the material world after killing the warden. When the soul falls in the embrace of her savior twin in a perfect, symbiotic ecstasy, their acquired freedom ends the rule of the cosmic usurpers. The archons are creatures of our minds, sustained by the humans' wasteful emotions. Once they are deprived of their nourishment, they vanish.

The other allegorical murder figuring in the gospel of Thomas was found in Logion 65, which also depicts a preemptive act against the intrusions of the archons and shows how our mind—described as the "son" of a powerful man—must be annihilated to make possible the eloping of the soul with her beloved.

The Mystical Family - Logion 99

> *The disciples said to him: "Your brothers and your mother are standing outside." He replied: "Those in these places here who do the will of my father, these are my brothers and my mother; they are the ones who will enter the mystical sovereignty of my father."*

Logion 55 enjoined us to renounce the earthly family as a cultural mechanism that serves the interests of worldly institutions but hinder the emancipation of the soul. But, from a transcendent standpoint, there is a figurative family in the heart of those who do the will of the invisible father and enter his mystical sovereignty (see also Logia 15, 44). The soul of the *pneumatici* is the mother of the living eidolon (see Logion 79), and she was fathered through the psychic thrust of the "I AM." The soul and the living eidolon are also siblings, twins in each other's image (see Logion 15). Father, mother, son, brother are all metaphorical aspects of the flow of pneuma as a family whose ties abide eternally in the form of a causal loop. The paradoxical role-playing of the divine essence and the dynamics created by its evolutionary manifestations confuse the rational mind but are the reality of the psychic thrust cycling in and out of time, space, and matter. This mystical if unconventional family manifested out of the "I AM" is strikingly depicted in another remarkable document discovered in Nag Hammadi alongside the gospel of Thomas. The vivid, short verses open our eyes to the peregrinations of the soul and the *syzygos*, which defy the traditional paradigm with intriguing paradoxes:

> ... I am the first and the last.
> I am the honored one and the scorned one.
> I am the whore and the holy one.
> I am the wife and the virgin.
> I am <the mother> and the daughter.
> I am the members of my mother.
> I am the barren one
> and many are her sons.
> I am she whose wedding is great,
> and I have not taken a husband.
> I am the midwife and she who does not bear.
> I am the solace of my labor pains.
> I am the bride and the bridegroom,
> and it is my husband who begot me.
> I am the mother of my father
> and the sister of my husband
> and he is my offspring.
> I am the slave of him who prepared me.

> *I am the ruler of my offspring.*
> *But he is the one who begot me before the time on a birthday.*
> *And he is my offspring in (due) time,*
> *and my power is from him.*
> *I am the staff of his power in his youth,*
> *and he is the rod of my old age.*
> *And whatever he wills happens to me.*

—From the *Thunder, Perfect Mind*, translated by George W. MacRae, excerpted from James M. Robinson, ed., The Nag Hammadi Library, revised edition. HarperCollins, San Francisco, 1990.

That which Belongs to the Rulers - Logion 100

> *They showed Jesus a gold piece, and they said to him, "Those who belong to Caesar demand taxes from us." He said to them: "Give to Caesar that which belongs to Caesar, to God that which belongs to God, and to me that which is mine."*

This saying is a more directly stated variation of Logion 81. Whatever our opinions on money and its usage might be, currencies flow through materialist institutions and serve materialistic impulses most. There is no way around the fact that we cannot aspire to leave the world of matter for the place of light without returning to the rulers—at least symbolically, through an applied detachment from all things material—the poisoned gifts they gave us. Our soul, on the other hand, belongs to the living eidolon, her savior twin with whom she must return to godhood.

The Two Families - Logion 101

> *"Whoever does not hate his [father] and his mother as I do cannot become a [disciple] to me; and whoever does [not] love his [father and] his mother as I do cannot become a [disciple] to me. My mother [...]; [my] true [mother], however, gave me the life."*

This part of the manuscript was damaged, and the saying is incomplete. However, we can recover the substance of Logion 101 with the help of Logia 55, 79 and 99. By now we understand how Thomas distinguishes between the institutionalized, earthly family and the figurative one. We must embrace the latter while renouncing and even hating the former. Although the stance may appear too radical and harsh, we should remember we are not referring to individuals but to a structure created with the purpose of serving the interests of the rulers and the archons:

- ensuring the perpetuation of our species in captivity

- keeping humans in a state of subservience to societies and cultural institutions
- controlling and enslaving humankind with the aim of holding the soul entrapped in matter and force the constant return of parcels of pneuma onto the physical plane.

The other family is the personification of stages and changes in the progression of pneuma. The human mother gives earthly life to a human child in this world, and that is a dubious gift. The unearthly mother, the soul, gives the gift of true life by conceiving the living eidolon who is to become her savior twin (see Logion 79).

Misplaced Loyalties - Logion 102

> Jesus said: "Woe to the Pharisees, because they resemble a dog resting upon the manger of the oxen; it does not eat, and it does not allow the oxen to eat."

The dog is the archetype of loyalty and does what its master commands. It is harrowing to watch deranged individuals ill-treating pets who still remain loyal to their abusers. Yet, that is a fitting allegory for the human condition: the hand that feeds us is also the hand that tyrannizes us, and we tolerate the rulers who gorge themselves with luxuries while other people suffer. Thus, the wealth of the world is concentrated within a few nations, and the wealth of a nation is in the hands of a few individuals. But beyond the world of injustice, Logion 102—as did Logion 39—points to a tragic paradox: those who willfully participate in the enslavement of their kind are slaves themselves. Indeed, tyrants understand that the most efficiently run prisons are those where a few inmates collaborate with the warders to police the other prisoners like dogs who do not eat and do not let the cattle eat either.

Resisting the Archons - Logion 103

> *Jesus said: "Blessed is the man who knows where the thieves are coming in so (that) he may arise and gather his [...] (household) and gird his loins early before they come in."*

We encountered the thieves in Logia 21 and 35: they are the archons who seek to keep the soul and her betrothed apart and prevent the strengthening of a bond between the two. They attack our minds to forestall the birth of the living eidolon and detain the divine essence. As we approach the last of Thomas' words of wisdom, this logion is a reminder to make good use of that which we learned and defend ourselves from the relentless assaults of our invisible enemies and those who willfully serve them (see Logion 102). With our foreknowledge, we are no longer hapless victims, unaware of the drama unfolding on the theatre of our mind. We know we have both a soul and a *syzygos*, and that our salvific liberation depends on the two becoming a monad. We can find repose in this blessed henosis when we stop listening to the voices of the world and turn to the inner regions of our being where there is strength, guidance, and, above all, the will that supersedes our own.

A Tragic Fate - Logion 104

> They told [Jesus]: "Come, let us pray today and fast." Jesus replied: "What is the sin I have done or in what have I been defeated? "Nevertheless, when the bridegroom comes out of the bridal chamber, then let them fast and let them pray."

Although Logion 6 stated that religious rites are mostly futile, the idea could not be impressed on the minds of the disciples, leaving the teacher so exasperated that he wonders aloud what he might have done wrong. Now his students want him to pray and fast with them instead of applying themselves to the examination of his wisdom. They do not see their obtuseness will continue to drive a wedge between their soul and her syzygos

The living eidolon makes his dwelling in the truthful heart where he woes the soul as her savior twin (Logion 75). Together, they will leave their bridal chamber at the moment of the physical death (Logion 59). Then, those who are still living in the world of the dead have sufficient reasons to fast and pray, more for themselves (see Logia 1 and 56) than for the departed who has risen to the empyrean of the blessed.

Child of the Soul - Logion 105

> *Jesus said: "He who will know the father and the mother will be referred to as the son of a harlot."*

Logion 105 is another startling saying that leaves the scholar and casual reader alike dumbfounded. But we have clues to help us understand this mysterious statement. From Logion 101 we can imply that "he who will know the father and mother" can distinguish between the construct of worldly family ties and the dynamics of the figurative family within. The living eidolon knows his mother is the soul (see Logion 79), and his father is the "I AM" (see Logion 15). In the *Exegesis of the Soul*, a gnostic manuscript found at Nag Hamadi alongside the *Gospel of Thomas*, the entanglements of the soul in the world of matter are allegorized as the descent of a woman into prostitution:

> *And in her body, she prostituted herself and gave herself to one and all, considering each one she was about to embrace to be her husband. When she had given herself to wanton, unfaithful adulterers, so that they might make use of her,*

> then she sighed deeply and repented. But even when she turns her face from those adulterers, she runs to others and they compel her to live with them and render service to them upon their bed, as if they were her masters. Out of shame she no longer dares to leave them, whereas they deceive her for a long time, pretending to be faithful, true husbands, as if they greatly respected her. And after all this they abandon her and go.

—Translated by William C. Robinson Jr., excerpted from The Nag Hammadi Library in English edited by James M. Robinson, and transcribed for online publication originally at the Gnostic Society Library [gnosis.org].

So far, we see how the soul is misled away from her legitimate companion (the *syzygos*). The Exegesis continues:

> From heaven the father sent her her man, who is her brother [see Logion 22], the firstborn. ... But then the bridegroom, according to the father's will, came down to her into the bridal chamber, which was prepared. And he decorated the bridal chamber.

The bridegroom, then, is the living eidolon, at once brother and husband (a common motif in mythology), but also the son of the soul who had become a harlot. A verse from the Thunder, Perfect Mind (see Logion 99) summarizes the painful journey of the soul through corruption and whoredom all the while preserving her divine quality:

> *I am the whore and the holy one.*

Hence, the living eidolon is "referred to as the son of a harlot" because the soul his mother is trapped in the flesh. In her aspect of the bride however, the soul is holy and escapes matter:

> *She gave up her former prostitution and cleansed herself of the pollutions of the adulterers, and she was renewed so as to be a bride. She cleansed herself in the bridal chamber; ... The soul then moves of her own accord. And she received the divine nature from the father for her rejuvenation, so that she might be restored to the place where originally she had been. This is the resurrection that is from the dead. This is the ransom from captivity. This is the upward journey of ascent to heaven.*

The Power of the Monad - Logion 106

> *Jesus said: "When you make the two a monad, you will become the sons of man, and if you tell this mountain (to) move away, it will move."*

Logion 106 confirms our interpretation of Logion 48 while reiterating the aphorism of "moving mountains." When the two—that is our soul and her savior twin—are made a monad, we become "sons of man" or in the likeness (see Logion 108) of the "son of man" (see Logion 86) who is the savior twin (see Logion 22). Soul and *syzygos*, the mystical twins have found each other at last. But it is not the end of the journey for the pair: when "the two are made a monad," the dyad collapses, and the twy-formed god is born with a might to move mountains.

The Lover and the Beloved - Logion 107

Jesus said: "The mystical sovereignty can be compared a shepherd who had a hundred sheep. The largest one strayed (from the flock), and he left the ninety-nine (sheep to) go after that one until he found it. Having gone to such trouble, he said to the sheep: 'I desire (†) you more than the ninety-nine (others).'"

Thomas depicts the dynamics between the soul and the *syzygo*s as the search of the lover for her beloved. In the parable of Logion 107, it is the bridegroom who finds his lost bride. The mystical sovereignty is not a locality (see Logion 3), but the dimension of bliss, ecstasy and creative capability the soul enters when she marries her eternal, heavenly companion. The mutual passions of the soul and the savior twin is allegorized in tales and myths such as the romance of Eros and Psyche wherein the young god finds his bride to be, wakes her from torpor, and takes her to Olympus where they would live as immortals.

We recall from Logion 105 that the soul's destiny can be compared to a descent into prostitution: like the allegorical sheep, she strays from the path. However, one is the "largest." She has a "truthful and believing heart" (††), which the living eidolon can fill with his presence. An individual soul is unique to a single lifetime whereas the pneuma journeys through myriad simultaneous cycles of time, to shepherd an unimaginable number of souls: they are "the ninety-nine" he left behind for the one he desired (†) more than the others because "his name was on her lips when he did not dwell with her" (††).

—

† Note how the shepherd is motivated by Desire (see Logia 15 and 75)

†† See Logion 59 for full quote.

The Likeness of the Savior Twin - Logion 108

Jesus said: "Whoever drinks out of my mouth will become like me; I myself will become like him, and that which is veiled will be unveiled to him."

This Logion once more implies the Jesus of Thomas is not a historical individual but the personification of the living eidolon within. Had the savior been a being of flesh and blood, it could be argued our likeness to him would be abstract (e.g. we become enlightened and pure as he is). If this were the case however, it is difficult to see why and how he would become like us.

When we drink from the mouth of the living eidolon, we heed the living water of gnosis (see Logion 74), and we give birth to our savior twin (see Logion 70), the revealer of "that which is veiled." Not only do the soul and her mystical twin look alike (see Logion 22), they are also interdependent: the soul is the liberator of her savior because without her the pneuma is bound to be plunged back into matter in search of his lover. Together, the lover and the beloved break the chains of physicality and find repose in the empyrean of the blessed.

The Descent into Materialism - Logion 109

> *Jesus said: "The mystical sovereignty can be compared to a man who unknowingly had a treasure [hidden] in his field and, [after] his death, he left it to his [son]. The son did not know (either). He took over the field (and) gave it [away]; [and] whoever bought it went plowing and [found] the treasure. He began to give money at interest to whom he loved."*

By the time the New Testament was edited, the parables of Jesus had assumed the familiar formula the reader might expect to find in the writings of Thomas as well. But some of Thomas' parables are unique, and others with a counterpart in the canonical gospels do not follow the traditional form. What is missing in the Thomasian tale of the hidden treasure is the typical resolution, the climatic surprise at the end of the story with its obvious moralistic implications, because Thomas wants us to think more deeply for ourselves and draw our own conclusions.

Logion 76 told the story of a merchant who reconsidered his priorities and sold his merchandise to buy a single pearl (a symbol of gnosis). He could easily have used his new acquisition to "give money at interest" but, instead, he kept the priceless discovery for the benefit of his soul. In his own narrative, Matthew amalgamates the parables of the pearl and of the hidden treasure (†) in such a way that they are made to carry an identical message. But in Thomas, the two stories are more developed and kept apart, with significantly different imports.

With Logion 109, we witness an irreversible descent into materialism. The three protagonists of the parable have something in common: they are materialists without connection to their inner life. The first person owns a field, which signifies he is engrossed in the material world (see Logion 21), unaware of the numinous treasure hidden (trapped) deep in matter. The owner's son inherits the field but is just as unaware of its concealed value. His interests are still materialistic, and he sells the land for profit. Then comes the buyer who represents the farthest rung down the ladder of materialism. In fact, he is the opposite of the trader we met in Logion 76. Here is a comparison of the two:

- The trader was looking for valuable merchandise; the buyer of the field found the treasure accidentally.
- The trader sells all he has to acquire the pearl; the buyer of the field seeks to profit financially.
- The trader keeps the pearl for himself; the buyer of the field gives to his love ones.
- The trader forgoes trading; the buyer of the field develops his business venture.

It might be tempting to attribute redeeming qualities to the industrious person (††) who, unlike his rather lazy predecessors, went through the trouble of plowing the field, but money (see Logia 63, 64) and usury (Logion 95) do not sit well with Thomas. Note also that the buyer of the field lends the money to whom he loved, suggesting the family ties Thomas loathes (see Logion 101). The fact is, if the two previous owners of the field did not know about the hidden treasure, the new buyer willfully ignores its intrinsic, spiritual value and is only interested in material gains.

So, how does the behavior of the three materialistic men can compare to the mystical sovereignty? It shows once more that the liberation of our divine essence is a gift most are not ready to receive. Mankind prefers to meander foolishly on all the wrong paths that lead farther away from the treasure nearby. The mystical sovereignty is everywhere (see Logion 3) but becomes a heavenly refuge (see Logion 20) only for the *pneumatici*, the chosen who heed gnosis and surrender to the sempiternal Desire within.

—

† Because Logion 109 looks like a garbled elaboration of Matthew 13: 44, some scholars assume the writer did not grasp the meaning of the original story and reworked it unsuccessfully to make it appear more significant. However, it is as likely that the Christian redactor-copyists who read Thomas were perplexed and rearranged the complex, hermetic metaphor into a simpler, moralistic parable that suited the Christian frame of reference.

†† This allows us to open a parenthesis with regard to the Calvinist assumption that industriousness is rewarded by God and is the mark of the elect. The ultimate, extreme outcome of this view is evidenced in the tragically skewed outlook of the believers in the "law of attraction" and proponents of a "prosperity theology" whose interests betray an obsession with acquisitions and dominion. They do not see the treasure in the field as a numinous end, but as a spiritual means to worldly ends. In that sense, they are anti-spiritual because they seek physical entanglements for their soul instead of striving to liberate the divine

essence. The scholar of esoterica Manly P. Hall remarked on this corruption of numinous sensitivity:

> *Though the demonism of the Middle Ages seems to have disappeared, there is abundant evidence that in many forms of modern thought—especially the so-called "prosperity" psychology, "willpower-building" metaphysics, and systems of "high-pressure" salesmanship—black magic has merely passed through a metamorphosis, and although its name be changed its nature remains the same.*

—Manly Palmer Hall, the *Secret Teachings of all Ages*.

Last Warning to the Materialists - Logion 110

> *Jesus said: "Whoever has found the world and become rich, let him renounce the world."*

Logion 110 combines Logia 80 and 81, collapsing them into one prime insight: a warning to those who are led down the path of materialism as previously described in Logion 109. They must renounce the world that made them rich! It is a radical pronouncement, but when we understand the overarching import of the gospel of Thomas, we know the life we live leads to only two alternatives: release of the soul or spiritual death.

The royalty and priestly elite in ancient societies such as the Celts, Vikings, Etruscans, or Egyptians wanted to be buried with all the implements they had enjoyed in their terrestrial abode, thinking they could take everything along into the next world. Things are not much different in our days when it seems impossible for the average person to part with his mobile phone for more than 20 minutes at a time. Far from renouncing our attachment to materiality, we are becoming more dependent on the rich variety of its dubious gifts.

A Promise to the Pneumatici - Logion 111

> *Jesus said: "The heavens will be rolled up, and the earth (too) before you, and he who lives out of the living one will not look (up)on death." Because Jesus speaks thus: "He who finds himself, of him the world is not worthy."*

The cosmos will not last forever but those who draw forth the living eidolon from within (see Logion 70) will have eternal life. Here the distinction is clearly made (see also note on Logion 0) between "the living one" within—the savior twin—and the one who is alive in a world that is dead (see Logion 56). Because the latter finds the former, he rises above the realm of matter that is not worthy of him.

The Flesh and the Soul - Logion 112

Jesus said: "Woe to the flesh that clings to the soul; woe to the soul that clings to the flesh."

We explained part of this logion in our elucidation of Logion 87: the soul is contingent on a physical body for her existence because the memories arise and are stored in the living tissues. This necessary constraint, however, will be lifted when the soul is taken into the etherealized body (see Logion 84) of the savior twin. But how can it be awful "for the flesh that clings to the soul?" We find the solution to this new riddle in Logion 6 that warns against the impediments we place on the flesh in the name of religion and, mistakenly, for the sake of the soul. Typically, the faithful adherents of the myriad congregations on earth are led to believe salvation is conditional, determined by the moral boundaries they place on natural compulsions. They summit the body to all sorts of rigors to purify the soul (see also Logion 68), and the first impulse they usually seek to regiment is the sex drive. The codification of sexual behaviors in societies can be almost uniquely attributed to religious factors or traced back to archaic taboos. Nations that claim to have built a wall of separation between state and religion need only to look at the sex laws on their books to see how they delude themselves. We let loose, and even encourage the aggression and greed instincts on many strata of the social system, but God forbid we would grant authentic sexual freedom for all or promote free love in our society. Notwithstanding the psychological benefits of naturism, mere public nudity is a punishable offense in industrialized and/or theocratic societies, and the male erection is considered de facto pornographic.

From the perspective of the dualist, just being on earth is detrimental and evil is rooted so deeply in matter, it cannot be rectified through the imposition of a moral conduct. The categorization of evil is always subjective, and only the soul who no longer clings to the flesh, having turned to the living eidolon within, if purified from all that which is detrimental to her.

Alternatively, the aphorism of the flesh and the soul is a reminder of the circular nature of reality (see Logion 18) and the unfortunate but necessary interdependency of the physical body, the psychic thrust, and the soul (see Logion 29) until the chosen is liberated at last.

* * *

The Latter-Day Saints are a curious instance of fervent believers who literally make the flesh depend on the soul. The Mormons enforce a ludicrous "Law of Chastity," perpetuate preposterous taboos, and have rigid requirements to attend services and performs various functions. Every deed is carefully monitored by the Elders, and the leaders have been clear in their pronouncements that breaking repeatedly even the smallest rule may endanger the "exaltation" of the individual. The reward for their lifetime dedication of subduing the flesh is, astonishingly, another body of flesh and bones (albeit "glorified") to house the spirit on a paradisiacal planet. Latter-Day Saints also perpetuate in the kingdom to come the same family ties they cultivated while on earth (see Logion 55). In other words, the Mormon soul forever "clings to the flesh."

Where the Mystical Sovereignty Is - Logion 113

> *His disciples asked him: "What day is the kingdom coming?"*
>
> *"It is not coming to be seen out there. No one will (be able to) say 'look in this or that direction.' Instead, the mystical sovereignty of the father is spread out upon the earth, and men are not looking upon it."*

The penultimate saying in the gospel of Thomas mirrors the words of Logion 3 at the beginning of the manuscript, and the disciples appear just as clueless now as they were the first time we found them asking the same basic questions. It is saddening to observe that after having received the keys to the realization of the mystical sovereignty, the disciples still do not see it before their eyes and carried embryonically in the heart of every human. For all the momentous revelation of the gospel of

Thomas, they have only been able to progress from the question of where the kingdom might be to an inquiry of when it might come. They have mistaken the injunction to never stop seeking gnosis (see Logion 2) for a suggestion to look and hope for a religious utopia.

Male Spirit, Female Soul - Logion 114

> *Simon Peter said to them: "Let Mary leave us, for women (are) not worthy of the life." Jesus replied: "Behold, I myself will lead her so that I might make her male, so she might also come to be a living spirit in your male likeness. For any woman making herself male will enter the heavenly mystical sovereignty."*

Many readers enjoy reading Thomas only to get offended upon reaching the very last saying. Yet, we should remember Logion 2 warned that when we find, we would be troubled. Perhaps this is the test to see if we are ready to "reign over the entirety." Even scholars make excuses, telling us Logion 114 is a later addition, and that it does not quite fit into the overall spirit of Thomas. Because the logion does not match that which many exponents of Thomas would like to hear from a proto-feminist Jesus, they reject these last words as unauthentic. They make the same mistake as the purists who are still looking for the unadulterated Gospel of Jesus, fallen from his lips, and couched intact on the papyrus. Evidently, the gospel of Thomas was redacted through time, and it is precisely that whole, final, syncretic, metaphysical product—the combined intellectual efforts of mystics and philosophers—that interests us, not the hypothetical, original, moralistic (and probably very boring) thoughts and precepts of an itinerant preacher.

Unsurprisingly, it is Peter—the bumbling apostle—who is making the inept remark that serves to introduce Thomas' final riddle. Peter thinks that women are not worthy of eternal life, but women and men alike are led by their respective savior twin into the mystical sovereignty.

The confluence of the soul and the *syzygos* is allegorized throughout the Logia as the wedding of a bride with her bridegroom. Thus, their ecstatic union is the unstated consummation of an etherealized sexual act. The soul loses herself in the embrace of her mystical companion, thereon she coalesces with him into an androgynous monad. Maleness and femaleness are esoteric functions attributed to the *syzygos* and the soul respectively (see Logion 22). All humans have a "female" soul who must leave the flesh to follow the "male" counterpart. Whereas in human sexuality the man penetrates his wife, the soul (our memories and individuality) is absorbed into the etherealized body of her consort, whereupon making the woman "manly" and "enter the heavenly mystical sovereignty."

APPENDIX 1: Jesus, Thomas, and the disciples

In the Logia of Thomas, Jesus is a tenuous figure. The only place where he figures prominently is at the beginning of each saying to introduce them. If we remove the instances of "Jesus said" from the text though, the content is not in any way weakened, and the logia can solidly stand on their own without reference to whomever spoke them. The sayings supposedly collected by Thomas were assembled from different traditions across time and then edited to fit a format that conveys a somewhat unified philosophy. The last needed touch was to give the collection of logia a seal of authority and an aura of holiness. If the other gospels draw their clout from the prominence of the apostles who allegedly wrote them and reminisced about their savior, the gospel of Thomas could raise the ante by being the words of Jesus himself spoken directly to the reader, placing itself audaciously above the competition in terms of preeminence and validity (†). The Thomasian Jesus, however, is not the solemn son of a god who dies and is resurrected, who performs miracles and redeems mankind from sin before coming back dramatically to life as the Christ. That mythological messiah of the synoptic gospels was crafted by Christian clerics based for the most part on the mythological dying solar gods of the ancient mystery cults. Indeed, the Christic journey can be regarded as a prototype of humankind's own search for its divine nature and ultimate ascension to godhood. Comparatively, the Jesus in Thomas, is a wandering preacher with little credentials and impressive claims of a mandate, who remains misunderstood by his followers except Thomas. This more archetypal than historical Jesus could have been one or an assemblage of the many holy prophets, doomsayers, agitators, and ascetic teachers who roamed the dusty roads of Palestine at the turn of the Current Era. The hierophant-Jesus we meet in Thomas, then, has a double persona, part literal, part figurative.

Thomas calls his hierophant figure the "living Jesus" as one who is spiritually awake and aware amidst a humanity who is mostly spiritually asleep or dead. It is also a subtle way to distinguish the enlightened teacher from the cult figure who must die ignominiously in order to be worshipped as God. Jesus the Wise shares his wisdom with a few select disciples (as opposed to the throngs in the canonical gospels), but even among them only a few understand the deeper meaning of their teacher's words. Thomas appears sharper and becomes privy to the most esoteric parts of the Jesus' canon he commits to write down for the posterity. Or so the story goes.

We should keep in mind that the "veiled words" are not so much what "Jesus said" but, more accurately, what Thomas said Jesus said. The name Thomas, of course, is a pseudonym for the real authors of the gospel, who preferred to withdraw behind their writings, attributing them to a legendary figure who could be remembered for the ages. Much like Plato exposes the teachings of Socrates to his students in a series of "dialogues," it is the anonymous authors of the gospel according to Thomas, and not Jesus, who speak to us from the remote past.

The selection of Thomas as the alleged writer of a gospel was not random. Because John describes him as someone who is not easily convinced and demands evidence (see John 20: 24-29), he embodies the admirable traits of the seeker who puts everything to test and will not rely on mere hearsays or blind faith. The Sufi mystic Al-Ghazali wrote:

> *Doubt transports you to the truth. Who does not doubt fails to inquire. Who does not inquire fails to gain insight. Without insight, you remain blind and perplexed.*

Thomas, familiarly known as "Doubting Thomas," personifies the profoundly self-reflecting individual who stands in contrast to the disciples who are easily impressed by the earthly charismatic teachers they invest with the authority to tell them things pleasing to their ears.

The wisdom of the Doubter gives us a choice: we can be Thomas, the skeptic who heeds gnosis as it streams unspoiled from its pellucid source; or we can be the disciples who accept edited and adulterated knowledge from the lips of whomever they decide to "like and follow" at a particular moment of their life.

Thomas is also the twin of Jesus (see Logion 0), which, again, is meant to be understood both literally and metaphorically. This takes us back to the unfolding of a Jesus myth that mirrors the actual, mystical developments in the core of our own being: the "living one" (the higher Self) is revealed to Thomas, his twin (the soul), while the obtuse disciples (the natural self or mind) remain blind to transcendent realities.

—

† The clever contraption works so well that even some modern scholars tend to see the gospel of Thomas as closer to the real deal (that is the words of Jesus mostly recorded as they fell from his own mouth) when compared to the canonical gospels.

APPENDIX 2: The Archons

Before mankind rose, the Archons did not exist. Yet, they are as eternal as we are in the circular nature of reality, being born of our disturbed subconscious. Whereas Pneuma, the breath of the god-being into whom we develop, engendered us, the human species engenders the archons through the exacerbated emotional states it exhibits. We unwittingly create them during our earthly sojourn with the powerful emotions that clog our subconscious as a part of the deep-seated legacy of our primal, dual disposition (Logion 7). The more we tamper with those emotions (as for example when we strive to suppress anger, create happiness, or deny "improper" desires), the stronger they grow until they discharge or sip externally, whereupon rise doppelgängers of a sort, driven by an imperative to self-manifest and survive. If the savior twin is an angel of light (the illuminating agent within us) for each individual soul, the archons can be thought of as the angels of the demiurge or the delusional parts of ourselves. Emotions are biochemical and electrical responses, and it is not inconceivable that they can affect and alter the physical environment outside our body. Whatever the mechanism might be, once the archons escape the confines of the mind (our dreams for instance), they take a life on their own in the supersubstantial regions that border the physical plane and start vying for our attention. The most evolved of the archons have the ability to assume the shapes of our cultural and experiential expectations and form a rough identity based on our individual and collective memories. They remain however purely material entities, without self-awareness, and lacking the psychic thrust that links the rest of the creation to the divine.

The Archons are fascinated by the human soul they do not have, and their existence becomes parasitic, sustained by our own psychic life on which they prey. Their domain is the cosmos, Earth, and the whole of the physical plane over which they rule and of which they are de facto guardians. Their mastery of matter allow them to shift appearances and move quickly in an out of sight in elusive fashion. The archonic powers are at the source of all paranormal phenomena and religious visitations.

The rulers and warders of the cosmos are also the ambassadors of Mother Nature: alternatively generous, cruel, possessive, occasionally evil, always self-serving and deceptive, dominated by their drive to survive. Without us there would be no them, and their interest lies in keeping us ensnared in matter. To that end, they control the paths that lead to the liberation of the divine essence, and they work tirelessly to foster the societal developments that serve their aims more effectively. They inevitably come into conflict with a procreancy of the spirit that seeks to beget that which is above nature. In effect, the archons are the thieves of the soul and the enemies of the *syzygos*. Yet, we must not fear them: the Archons are an integral part of ourselves, and, as we bring our attention closer to our ethereal component, they progressively fade and vanish in the end, yielding to the triumph of the savior twin.

GLOSSARY

APEIRON the "boundless." A lyrical term ascribed to that which underlies the whole or everything that is. See also "field," and "tide of Apeiron."

DEMIURGE. A mythological figure who personifies the false god, ruler of the cosmos and leader of the archons. Represents the shackles of matter as he stands to keep the divine essence under his control on the material plane.

DESIRE. With a capital "D." The primal cause worshipped by the ancients as Eros Protogenos. The self-sustaining intent of the "I AM." God in the most abstract sense.

DIVINE ESSENCE. That which is often, imprecisely referred to as "spirit." The presence of the divine into matter, manifesting itself under different forms aspects from the "pneuma," to the soul-*syzygos* dyad.

DYAD, DYADIC, DYADICITY. Refer to the split nature of our divine essence, which consists in the soul and the *syzygos* pair, separate and distinct from each other; whereas "dual" and "duality" refer in my writings to the two opposite principles active in matter: the psychic thrust and entropy.

EIDOLON. The reflection of the soul in the innermost, which becomes a living image and subsequently the savior twin of the soul. Once the psychic thrust has reached its aim in the birth of the soul, the soul in turn has the ability to fold back upon herself and imprint her reflection on the field of Apeiron. The soul's longing further shapes her image into the living eidolon.

EMPYREAN OF THE BLESSED. The repose of the soul and her mystical twin. A dimension beyond space and time, free from all conceivable constraints except that of necessity. The abode of the god-being. See also "Pleroma."

FIELD OF APEIRON. The realm of possibilities. The dimension of the Apeiron where all that can conceivably be already exist in latent form, waiting to be dreamed or set in motion.

GNOSTICI. A gnostic term referring to those who have received, understood, and applied the salvific knowledge (Greek *gnosis*) in their lives. Used alternatively for *pneumatici* in this book.

HENOSIS. The transcendent confluence or mystical wedding of the soul and the savior twin. The process of becoming a monad.

HYLICI. A gnostic term (from the Greek *hylē*, the matter) referring to those who have no concern for or belief in the transcendental aspects of their being. They are generally engrossed in matter and more interested in worldly affairs than in the numinous.

"I AM." Our divine aspect. The dreamer and the dream, the observer and that which is observed. The self-reflecting god, at once himself and the other throughout its self-sustaining cycle.

MONAD. The transcendent state of oneness with the divine. The confluence of the soul and the savior twin. In contrast to the dyad formed by the *syzygos* and the soul who have yet to merge.

PLEROMA. A gnostic term meaning "fullness" or "plenitude." It is the "place of light" described by Thomas that I call the "empyrean of the blessed," where the soul finds eternal repose with her divine companion.

PNEUMA. The divine breath. A metaphor for the power of the divinity. Pneuma insufflates matter, and souls can be described as parcels of pneuma trapped in the flesh.

PNEUMATICI. A gnostic term (from the Greek "pneuma," the divine breath) referring to the chosen, or elect: those who have renounced the outside world and turned to the divine essence within.

PSYCHIC THRUST. Sempiternal Desire carried through pneuma onto the material plane. The outcome of the psychic thrust is the formation of one's soul.

PSYCHICI. A gnostic term (from the Greek *psychē*, the soul) referring to those who seek salvation for their soul but are lost on the endless pathways of religions and spiritual movements. They would sooner turn to religious leader and spiritual teachers than trust the intimations from within.

PULL OF STASIS. The entropic principle within the tide of Apeiron, pitted against the divine psychic thrust.

RULER(S). Broadly speaking, every living entity who has the power to exert control over the destiny of a fellow being. In that sense, we all are rulers and participants in maintaining the structure of society, the human superorganism from which we hope to benefit somehow. More narrowly as it applies to gnostic thought and the gospel of Thomas, the rulers are the Archons (see Appendix 2) who have a vested interest in supporting the cultural and social institutions that hinder the liberation of the soul. The segment of the population we may call the "powers that be" or the "establishment" in modern parlance are also the unwitting (although there may also be a willful collusion between some authorities and the occult guardians of the cosmos) accomplices of the Archons in sustaining the social framework. However, it would be a mistake to blame all the ills and troubles of life on a secretive elite of powerful politicians, religious leaders, and financiers bent on enslaving the world. The truth is we all have a share of responsibility in forging the shackles that bind us.

SAVIOR TWIN. The savior of the soul. The highest aspect of the *syzygos*. A divine, etherealized being whose shape and characteristics flow from the soul's desire. In mysticism, he is described as the Beloved whose lover is the soul.

SOUL. The experiential memories of a lifetime, which give us our sense of individuality. Memories are information and, as such, the soul has no existence apart from a physical body unless it is snatched by the *syzygos* when the flesh perishes and decays.

SPIRIT. A word that is so overused in modern parlance, it has ceased to carry any meaning. Worse yet, it is often taken to mean the soul whereas the two are clearly distinct. Consequently, I only use "spirit" when I quote from Thomas, or the Christian scriptures.

STASIS. The condition of the field of Apeiron in its unmoved state; unrealized potential; unmanifested cycles of reality.

SUPERSUBSTANTIAL. Refers to the intangible region and quality of matter.

TIDE OF APEIRON. Lyrical expression for the surge of a new cycle of reality within Apeiron. Inherent to the tide are both its life giving and destructive powers: the psychic thrust and the entropic principle.

TWY-FORMED GOD. The metaphorical "holy child" of the soul and the savior twin, who is the god formed by the soul and her consort. The prefix "twi-" means "double, as in twin." My use of the old English "twy-" is a personal choice owing to the shape of the letter "Y" symbolizing divergence and convergence.

SYZYGOS. The mystical "otherness" sought by the soul to reach the "I AM." That with which humans seek to connect through sexuality, romantic love, parental devotion, altruistic endeavors, etc. Both the living eidolon and the savior twin are aspects of the *syzygos*.

Made in the USA
Columbia, SC
17 May 2020